Django and Flask for Web Development

Python Frameworks Made Easy
Develop powerful, scalable web
apps using Python's top
frameworks

THOMPSON CARTER

Table of Content

TABLE OF CONTENTS

5

9

Introduction

Welcome to *"Mastering Web Development with Django and Flask: A Comprehensive Guide for Building Scalable, Secure, and AI-Powered Web Applications."*

The landscape of web development has evolved rapidly in recent years. With an ever-growing demand for dynamic, interactive, and scalable web applications, developers need tools that are not only powerful but also flexible and easy to learn. **Django** and **Flask**, two of the most popular Python web frameworks, have emerged as go-to solutions for developers seeking to build modern, secure, and high-performance web applications.

This book aims to provide a **comprehensive, in-depth guide** to web development using Django and Flask. Whether you are a beginner eager to explore the world of Python web development or an experienced developer looking to enhance your skills, this book is tailored to meet your needs.

In this book, we'll dive into the essentials of both **Django** and **Flask**, exploring their strengths, use cases, and how they complement each other in different web development scenarios. We'll provide detailed examples and hands-on tutorials to equip you with the knowledge necessary to build and deploy real-world applications with ease.

What You'll Learn:

1. Django and Flask Fundamentals:

We'll begin by introducing you to both Django and Flask, comparing their strengths and weaknesses. You'll learn which framework is best suited for your project needs, whether you're building a full-fledged, data-driven application (Django) or a lightweight, modular web service (Flask). You'll master the core components of both frameworks, including **routing**, **views**, **templates**, and **models**, along with how to handle **user authentication** and **form validation**.

2. Advanced Features and Best Practices:

As we progress, we'll dive into more advanced topics, such as:

- **Database management** and ORM in Django/Flask
- **Caching** and performance optimization

- **Security**: How to protect your web applications from common vulnerabilities
- **Real-Time Applications**: Integrating WebSockets and Django Channels for instant communication in your apps
- **API Development**: Building robust RESTful APIs using Django Rest Framework (DRF) and Flask
- **Machine Learning and AI**: Deploying ML models with Django and Flask to power your applications with artificial intelligence

3. Full-Stack Development:

Learn how to integrate **React** and **Vue** with Django and Flask to create full-stack web applications. You'll discover how to set up seamless communication between your frontend and backend using REST APIs and GraphQL, and how to deploy these modern apps to production.

4. Real-World Examples:

In this book, we've included **real-world examples** to help you understand how to apply the concepts you learn in practical scenarios. From creating a simple blog app to building complex, machine-learning-powered platforms, the examples will give you the confidence to tackle your own projects.

5. Career Development and Future Trends:

As web development continues to grow and evolve, this book also provides insight into the **future trends** of Python web frameworks. We'll explore emerging technologies such as **serverless architectures**, **microservices**, and **AI integration**, helping you stay ahead in the ever-changing tech landscape. Additionally, we'll offer guidance on **career opportunities** and **learning paths** to help you become a professional Django/Flask developer and land your dream job.

Why This Book?

For Beginners:

If you're new to web development, this book provides a **step-by-step guide** to understanding both Django and Flask from the ground up. We break down complex topics into manageable, easy-to-understand sections, providing ample explanations and code examples to guide you through each concept. By the end of the book, you'll be able to confidently create fully functional web applications using Django and Flask.

For Experienced Developers:

For those with some web development experience, this book serves as a valuable **reference guide** to Django and Flask, offering insights into advanced features like **database optimization**, **API development**, and **real-time communication**. We also provide best practices and modern development techniques that will help you improve your coding style, scalability, and security knowledge.

Practical, Hands-On Learning:

Each chapter of this book is designed to be **hands-on**, allowing you to follow along with the examples and build real applications as you go. You will not only learn the theory but also how to implement these concepts in real-world projects. This practical approach will ensure that you develop a strong understanding of web development that you can apply immediately in your own work.

How to Use This Book:

The structure of this book is designed to cater to both beginners and more experienced developers. You can approach the book in several ways:

1. **Follow the chapters sequentially**: This will guide you through the complete process of learning both Django and Flask, starting from the basics to more advanced topics like deploying AI-powered applications.
2. **Pick specific chapters**: If you're already familiar with the basics of Django or Flask, feel free to skip ahead to the chapters that focus on more advanced topics, such as integrating machine learning, building APIs, or deploying applications.
3. **Refer back as needed**: The book also serves as a **reference manual**, allowing you to revisit sections when you need guidance on specific topics or solutions to common problems.

Final Words:

Web development is an exciting, ever-evolving field, and Django and Flask are powerful tools that can help you build anything from simple websites to complex, high-performance web applications. Whether you are just starting out or looking to take your skills to the next level, *"Mastering Web Development with Django and Flask"* will guide you through the process of mastering these frameworks and help you build your own dynamic, scalable, and secure applications.

Let's get started on this journey to becoming an expert in web development with Django and Flask

PART 1

INTRODUCTION TO WEB DEVELOPMENT WITH PYTHON

CHAPTER 1

WHY PYTHON FOR WEB DEVELOPMENT?

Python has become one of the most **popular** and **versatile** programming languages, making it an **excellent choice** for web development. In this chapter, we'll explore **why Python** is widely used in the web development space, how Django and Flask fit into the ecosystem, and how Python compares to other web technologies. We'll also guide you through **setting up your development environment** so you're ready to start building web applications.

1.1 Overview of Python's Role in Web Development

Python is **widely used** in web development due to its **simplicity, readability, and efficiency**. Some of the key reasons why developers prefer Python for web applications include:

- **Easy to Learn & Use** – Python has a clean and intuitive syntax, making it beginner-friendly.

- **Large Community & Support** – A vast global community contributes to extensive libraries and frameworks.
- **Versatility** – It can be used for **backend development, data science, AI, automation, and more**.
- **Rapid Development** – Python's frameworks simplify web development by reducing repetitive tasks.
- **Scalability** – Many large-scale applications, including Instagram and Spotify, rely on Python.

Examples of Web Applications Built with Python

- **Instagram** – Uses Django to manage millions of users efficiently.
- **Pinterest** – Django helps handle vast amounts of user-generated content.
- **Netflix** – Uses Python for data analytics and backend services.

Python allows developers to create **dynamic, data-driven applications** while ensuring security, speed, and maintainability.

1.2 Why Choose Django or Flask?

Python offers several **web frameworks**, but **Django** and **Flask** are the most widely used. Choosing between them depends on the **type of project** and **development needs**.

Django: The Full-Stack Framework

Django is a **batteries-included** framework, meaning it provides built-in features for common web development tasks. It's ideal for large-scale applications that require **security, scalability, and rapid development**.

Advantages of Django

Built-in admin panel for easy management. **ORM (Object-Relational Mapping)** for handling databases efficiently. **Security features** such as CSRF and SQL injection protection. **Faster development** with reusable components.

Best for: Large-scale applications, e-commerce sites, and content-heavy platforms.

Flask: The Micro-Framework

Flask is **lightweight and flexible**, making it perfect for small applications and APIs. It gives developers more **freedom** to choose third-party tools and customize their projects.

Advantages of Flask

Minimalistic – Only provides essentials like routing and request   handling.

Highly customizable – Use any database, authentication system,   or   template   engine.

Great for APIs – Flask is a top choice for developing RESTful   APIs.

Faster for small projects – No unnecessary overhead.

Best for: Small projects, APIs, and microservices.

Choosing Between Django and Flask:

- Need a **quick, feature-rich** framework? → **Use Django.**
- Want **lightweight and flexible** development? → **Use Flask.**
- Working on an **API or microservice?** → **Flask is a great fit.**

1.3 How Python Compares to Other Web Development Languages

While **Python** is a strong contender in web development, other languages like **JavaScript, PHP, and Ruby** also play key roles.

Feature	Python	JavaScript	PHP	Ruby
Ease of Use	Simple & beginner-friendly	Complex for beginners	Easy but outdated	Readable but niche
Speed	Good performance	Fast	Slower than Python	Fast but less popular
Scalability	High (Django/Flask)	High (Node.js)	Moderate	Moderate
Best Use Cases	APIs, full-stack apps	Frontend & backend	CMS, blogs	Web apps

30

Feature	Python	JavaScript	PHP	Ruby
Security	Strong	Weaker by default	Prone to vulnerabilities	Secure

Why Python Wins:

- **Better readability** and **maintainability**.
- **More powerful frameworks** for modern web development.
- **Higher security and scalability** compared to PHP and Ruby.
- **Strong ecosystem** for AI, automation, and data science.

1.4 Setting Up Your Development Environment

Before we start building applications, let's set up your environment. You'll need:

1. Install Python

Ensure you have **Python 3.8 or later** installed. Check your version by running:

```sh
sh
```

```sh
python --version
```

If you don't have Python installed, download it from python.org.

2. Set Up a Virtual Environment

A **virtual environment** helps isolate dependencies for each project.

```sh
sh
```

```sh
# Install virtualenv if you haven't
pip install virtualenv

# Create a virtual environment
virtualenv myproject

# Activate it
# On Windows:
myproject\Scripts\activate

# On macOS/Linux:
source myproject/bin/activate
```

3. Install Flask and Django

Now, install both frameworks:

```sh
pip install django flask
```

4. Set Up a Basic Project

To create a **Django project**:

```sh

django-admin startproject my_django_app
cd my_django_app
python manage.py runserver
```

To create a **Flask project**:

```sh

# Create a file called app.py
touch app.py

# Open app.py and add:
from flask import Flask
app = Flask(__name__)

@app.route('/')
def home():
    return "Hello, Flask!"
```

```
# Run the app
if __name__ == '__main__':
    app.run(debug=True)
```

Run the Flask app:

```sh
sh
```

```
python app.py
```

You'll see **"Hello, Flask!"** when you open **http://127.0.0.1:5000/** in your browser.

Conclusion

In this chapter, we covered: **Why Python is great for web development**
Django vs. Flask – when to use each
How Python compares to other languages
Setting up your development environment

Now that your environment is ready, in the next chapter, we'll **explore web frameworks** in more detail!

34

CHAPTER 2

UNDERSTANDING WEB FRAMEWORKS

Web development involves handling multiple aspects, from managing requests and processing data to rendering web pages and interacting with databases. **Web frameworks** simplify this process by providing a structured way to build web applications.

In this chapter, we'll explore:

- What a web framework is and why it's useful
- The difference between **full-stack** and **micro** frameworks
- How frameworks help developers build efficient applications
- When to use **Django** vs. **Flask**

2.1 What is a Web Framework?

A **web framework** is a collection of tools, libraries, and pre-written code that helps developers create web applications efficiently. Instead of manually handling every aspect of a

35

web app, frameworks provide built-in solutions for common tasks such as:

Routing – Mapping URLs to functions that process requests

Database Management – Querying and storing data using Object-Relational Mapping (ORM)

Security – Protecting applications from vulnerabilities like SQL injection and CSRF attacks

Form Handling – Processing user input and validating data

Session & Authentication Management – Managing user logins and sessions

Why Use a Web Framework?

Without a framework, developers would have to write a lot of boilerplate code just to handle basic tasks like URL routing, handling HTTP requests, or interacting with a database. Frameworks save time by providing **pre-built modules**, reducing **code duplication**, and enforcing **best practices**.

Example Without a Framework (Manually Handling an HTTP Request):

```
python
```

36

```
import socket

server_socket   =   socket.socket(socket.AF_INET,
socket.SOCK_STREAM)
server_socket.bind(("localhost", 8080))
server_socket.listen(5)

while True:
    client_socket,          address          =
server_socket.accept()
    request = client_socket.recv(1024).decode()
    response = "HTTP/1.1 200 OK\n\nHello, World!"
    client_socket.sendall(response.encode())
    client_socket.close()
```

The above code handles a basic HTTP request **without** using a framework—it's tedious and inefficient. Now, compare this with **Flask**:

```python
from flask import Flask

app = Flask(__name__)

@app.route("/")
def home():
    return "Hello, World!"
```

```
if __name__ == "__main__":
    app.run(debug=True)
```

Flask automatically handles HTTP requests, responses, and server setup—with just a few lines of code!

2.2 Differences Between Full-Stack and Micro Frameworks

Web frameworks can be classified into two categories:

1. Full-Stack Frameworks (e.g., Django)

A **full-stack** framework provides all the tools needed to build a complete web application, including:

Built-in Admin Panel – Helps manage content and users without extra code
ORM (Object-Relational Mapping) – Simplifies database interactions
Form Handling & Authentication – User authentication and form validation tools
Security Features – Protection against SQL injection, CSRF, and more

Example: Django   Admin   Panel

Once you set up a Django project, you get an **admin panel** for free:

```sh
```

```
python manage.py createsuperuser
python manage.py runserver
```

Access **http://127.0.0.1:8000/admin/**, log in, and you have a full database management interface!

Pros of Full-Stack Frameworks

Best   for   **large-scale   applications**

Enforces **structured coding** and **security best practices**

Saves time with **pre-built features**

Cons of Full-Stack Frameworks

More   complex   and   **less   flexible**

Heavier than micro-frameworks

---

2. Micro Frameworks (e.g., Flask)

A **micro framework** provides only the **essential features** needed for web development. Developers can add libraries as required.

Minimal Features in Flask

No   built-in   admin   panel
No   default   ORM   (but   can   use   SQLAlchemy)
Lightweight and customizable

Pros of Micro Frameworks

Lightweight – Minimal dependencies, faster performance
Highly flexible – Choose only the tools you need
Best for APIs and microservices

Cons of Micro Frameworks

Requires **more manual setup** (e.g., authentication, admin panel)
Not ideal for **large-scale applications**

Feature	Django (Full-Stack)	Flask (Micro-Framework)
Built-in Admin Panel	Yes	No
Database ORM	Django ORM	Requires SQLAlchemy
Authentication	Built-in	Needs Flask-Login
Flexibility	Less flexible	Highly flexible
Best for	Large applications	Small projects & APIs

2.3 How Frameworks Simplify Development

Using a **framework** speeds up web development by providing **pre-built tools and organized structure**. Here's how:

1. Faster Development

- Frameworks **automate repetitive tasks** (e.g., form validation, security).
- Instead of writing custom authentication, **Django provides user authentication out of the box**.

41

2. Better Code Organization

- Frameworks **enforce structured programming**, making the codebase **easier to maintain**.
- Django follows the **Model-View-Template (MVT)** pattern:
  o **Model** (Database structure)
  o **View** (Business logic)
  o **Template** (HTML rendering)

3. Security Best Practices

- Django and Flask help protect against **common vulnerabilities** such as: **SQL Injection** (Prevented by ORM) **Cross-Site Scripting (XSS) Cross-Site Request Forgery (CSRF)**

4. Scalability & Performance

- **Django is great for high-traffic applications** (e.g., Instagram, Spotify).
- **Flask is better suited for lightweight, fast microservices** (e.g., Uber's API services).

2.4 When to Use Django vs. Flask?

Use Django If:

You're building a **large-scale, database-heavy** application. You need built-in features like **authentication, ORM, and admin** panel. Security and structure are a top priority.

Example Projects:

- Social Media Platforms (e.g., Instagram)
- E-commerce Websites (e.g., Shopify alternatives)
- Large Enterprise Applications

Use Flask If:

You need a **lightweight** and **customizable** solution. You're building an **API** or **microservice**. You prefer **full control over your tech stack**.

Example Projects:

- RESTful APIs (e.g., Backend for Mobile Apps)
- Microservices (e.g., Payment Processing API)

- Prototyping Quick MVPs

Decision Guide:

Scenario	Django	Flask
Full Web App (Admin, Authentication, Database)	Best choice	Requires extra setup
Microservice or API Backend	Too heavy	Lightweight and ideal
Custom, highly flexible project	Less flexible	Perfect for customization
Rapid Development & Security	Secure and fast	Requires manual security setup

Conclusion

In this chapter, we covered:
What web frameworks are and why they are useful
Differences between full-stack (Django) and micro-frameworks (Flask)
How frameworks simplify development
When to use Django vs. Flask

Now that you understand **web frameworks**, the next chapter will walk you through **setting up Django and Flask projects** to start building real-world applications!

CHAPTER 3

SETTING UP FLASK AND DJANGO PROJECTS

Before diving into web development with **Flask** and **Django**, you need to set up your environment properly. In this chapter, you'll learn:

How to install Flask and Django
Creating virtual environments to manage dependencies
Understanding project structures for both frameworks
Writing and running a simple Flask and Django app

By the end of this chapter, you'll have both a **Flask and Django project running locally** on your system.

3.1 Installing Flask and Django

To begin, make sure you have **Python 3.8 or later** installed on your machine. You can check your Python version by running:

sh

```
python --version
```

or

```
sh
```

```
python3 --version
```

If you don't have Python installed, download it from python.org.

Installing Flask and Django

Both Flask and Django can be installed using `pip` (Python's package manager). Run the following commands:

```
sh
```

```
pip install flask django
```

To verify the installation:

```
sh
```

```
python -m flask --version
python -m django --version
```

3.2 Creating Virtual Environments

A **virtual environment** helps isolate dependencies, ensuring your Flask and Django projects don't interfere with other Python projects. It allows you to install and manage specific versions of libraries.

Step 1: Install `virtualenv` (If not already installed)

sh

```
pip install virtualenv
```

Step 2: Create a Virtual Environment

Navigate to your project directory and run:

sh

```
# Create a virtual environment
virtualenv venv
```

For macOS/Linux:

sh

```
source venv/bin/activate
```

48

For Windows:

```sh
```

```sh
venv\Scripts\activate
```

Once activated, your command prompt should look like this:

```sh
```

```sh
(venv) $
```

Now you can install Flask or Django inside this isolated environment.

```sh
```

```sh
pip install flask
pip install django
```

To deactivate the virtual environment, use:

```sh
```

```sh
deactivate
```

3.3 Understanding Project Structures

Both **Flask** and **Django** organize their projects differently. Understanding their structures is essential before starting a real-world project.

Flask Project Structure (Minimalistic)

Flask doesn't impose a structure, but a common convention is:

csharp

```
flask_project/
|— app.py                # Main application file
|— static/                 # Static assets (CSS,
JavaScript, images)
|— templates/            # HTML templates
|— venv/                 # Virtual environment
└— requirements.txt   # List of dependencies
```

 Flask allows flexibility—you can structure the project however you prefer.

Django Project Structure (More Organized)

Django automatically creates a well-structured project:

```
graphql


django_project/
|— manage.py            # Entry point to run Django
commands
|— django_project/      # Main project directory
|     |— __init__.py     # Marks as a package
|     |— settings.py     # Configuration settings
|     |— urls.py         # URL routing
|     |— wsgi.py         # Web server entry point
|— app/                 # A Django app (e.g., blog,
user management)
|     |— models.py       # Database models
|     |— views.py         # Logic for handling
requests
|     |— templates/      # HTML templates
|     |— static/         # CSS/JS files
|     |— urls.py         # URL patterns specific to
this app
|— venv/                # Virtual environment
└— requirements.txt     # List of dependencies
```

Django enforces a **structured approach**—this makes scaling and maintaining apps easier.

3.4 Writing and Running a Simple Flask and Django App

3.4.1 Creating a Simple Flask App

Step 1: Create a File (`app.py`)

Inside your Flask project directory, create a file called `app.py` and add:

python

```
from flask import Flask

app = Flask(__name__)

@app.route("/")
def home():
    return "Hello, Flask!"

if __name__ == "__main__":
    app.run(debug=True)
```

Step 2: Run the Flask App

sh

```
python app.py
```

You'll see output similar to:

csharp

```
* Running on http://127.0.0.1:5000/
```

Step 3: Open in Browser

Go to **http://127.0.0.1:5000/** in your browser. You should see:

```
Hello, Flask!
```

Congratulations! You've just created your first Flask web app.

3.4.2 Creating a Simple Django App

Step 1: Create a Django Project

Navigate to your project directory and run:

```sh
```

```
django-admin startproject django_project
cd django_project
```

Step 2: Run the Django Development Server

```sh
```

```
python manage.py runserver
```

This starts a local server:

```
nginx
```

```
Starting         development         server         at
http://127.0.0.1:8000/
```

Step 3: Open in Browser

Go to **http://127.0.0.1:8000/** in your browser. You should see Django's default **"It worked!"** page.

3.4.3 Creating a Simple Django View

To display a custom message, modify `views.py` inside a new Django app.

Step 1: Create an App

Inside your Django project, run:

```
sh
```

```
python manage.py startapp myapp
```

Django will create a folder named `myapp/` with files like `views.py`.

Step 2: Modify `views.py`

Edit `myapp/views.py`:

python

```
from django.http import HttpResponse

def home(request):
    return HttpResponse("Hello, Django!")
```

Step 3: Configure URLs

Edit `django_project/urls.py` and **add the home route**:

python

```
from django.contrib import admin
from django.urls import path
from myapp.views import home

urlpatterns = [
    path('admin/', admin.site.urls),
    path('', home),
]
```

Step 4: Run the Server Again

sh

```
python manage.py runserver
```

Step 5: Visit `http://127.0.0.1:8000/`

Now you should see:

```
Hello, Django!
```

Great job! You've successfully created a basic Django app.

Conclusion

In this chapter, we covered: **Installing Flask and Django Setting up virtual environments Understanding Flask vs. Django project structures Writing and running simple Flask and Django applications**

With your projects set up, in the next chapter, we'll **dive deeper into Flask's core functionalities!**

CHAPTER 4

FLASK BASICS – ROUTING, VIEWS, AND TEMPLATES

Flask is a **lightweight and flexible** micro-framework that allows you to quickly build web applications with minimal setup. Unlike Django, which provides a full-stack solution, Flask focuses on **simplicity and flexibility**, allowing you to choose your own tools.

In this chapter, you'll learn:
How Flask's architecture works
Creating routes and handling requests
Working with Jinja2 templates for dynamic content

4.1 Understanding Flask's Minimalistic Architecture

Flask follows a **modular design**, meaning you only import and use what you need. At its core, Flask provides:

Routing – Mapping URLs to functions
Request Handling – Processing HTTP requests (GET,

POST,   etc.)

Template Rendering – Using Jinja2 for dynamic HTML

Session & Cookie Management – Handling user sessions

Extensibility – Easily add databases, authentication, and more

Flask vs. Django: Architecture Comparison

Feature	Flask (Micro-Framework)	Django (Full-Stack)
Flexibility	High – Choose your own tools	Less – Uses built-in features
Project Size	Best for small to medium apps	Best for large-scale apps
Built-in Features	Minimal – Need to install extras	Includes ORM, Admin, Auth
Learning Curve	Easier for beginners	Steeper learning curve

Flask is best suited for:

- **APIs & Microservices**
- **Prototyping & MVPs**

- **Small to Medium Web Apps**

4.2 Creating Routes and Handling Requests

A **route** in Flask maps a **URL to a function**. When a user visits a URL, Flask executes the associated function and returns a response.

4.2.1 Writing Your First Flask Route

Inside your Flask project, open `app.py` and add:

```python
from flask import Flask

app = Flask(__name__)

@app.route("/")
def home():
    return "Hello, Flask!"

if __name__ == "__main__":
    app.run(debug=True)
```

Run the app:

```sh
sh
```

```
python app.py
```

You'll see:

```csharp
csharp
```

```
 * Running on http://127.0.0.1:5000/
```

Visit **http://127.0.0.1:5000/** and see **"Hello, Flask!"** displayed.

4.2.2 Handling Multiple Routes

You can define multiple routes for different pages.

```python
python
```

```python
@app.route("/")
def home():
    return "Welcome to the Home Page!"

@app.route("/about")
def about():
    return "This is the About Page."
```

```
@app.route("/contact")
def contact():
    return "Contact us at contact@example.com"
```

Now, visiting **http://127.0.0.1:5000/about** will display:

```
csharp
```

```
This is the About Page.
```

4.2.3 Handling Dynamic URLs

You can capture parts of the URL as variables.

```
python
```

```
@app.route("/user/<username>")
def greet_user(username):
    return f"Hello, {username}!"
```

Visiting **http://127.0.0.1:5000/user/Alex** will return:

```
Hello, Alex!
```

More Examples of URL Variables:

```
python
```

```
@app.route("/post/<int:post_id>")
def show_post(post_id):
    return f"Post ID: {post_id}"
```

- **<int:post_id>** ensures only numbers are accepted.
- Visiting **http://127.0.0.1:5000/post/10** returns **"Post ID: 10"**.

4.2.4 Handling Different HTTP Methods

By default, routes accept **GET requests**, but Flask allows **POST, PUT, DELETE, etc.**

```python
from flask import request

@app.route("/submit", methods=["GET", "POST"])
def submit():
    if request.method == "POST":
        return "Form Submitted!"
    return "Send a POST request to submit."
```

If a **GET request** is made to /submit, it returns:

```css
```

Send a POST request to submit.

If a **POST request** is sent, it returns:

css

Form Submitted!

4.3 Working with Jinja2 Templates

Flask uses **Jinja2**, a templating engine that allows you to insert **dynamic content** into HTML.

4.3.1 Setting Up Templates

1. **Create a folder named `templates/`** in your Flask project.
2. **Inside `templates/`, create a file `index.html`** with the following content:

html

```
<!DOCTYPE html>
<html>
<head>
    <title>Flask App</title>
</head>
<body>
```

```
    <h1>Welcome, {{ name }}!</h1>
</body>
</html>
```

3. **Modify `app.py` to render the template:**

```python
python

from flask import Flask, render_template

app = Flask(__name__)

@app.route("/hello/<name>")
def hello(name):
    return        render_template("index.html",
name=name)
```

4. **Run the app** and visit **http://127.0.0.1:5000/hello/Alex**
   It will display:

```
Welcome, Alex!
```

4.3.2 Using Conditionals in Templates

Jinja2 allows **if-else conditions** inside templates.

```
html
```

```
{% if name == "Admin" %}
    <h1>Welcome, Administrator!</h1>
{% else %}
    <h1>Welcome, {{ name }}!</h1>
{% endif %}
```

4.3.3 Using Loops in Templates

You can loop through lists in Jinja2.

Modify app.py:

python

```
@app.route("/users")
def users():
    user_list = ["Alice", "Bob", "Charlie"]
    return          render_template("users.html",
users=user_list)
```

Create templates/users.html:

html

```
<!DOCTYPE html>
<html>
<head>
    <title>Users</title>
```

65

```
</head>
<body>
    <h1>Registered Users</h1>
    <ul>
        {% for user in users %}
            <li>{{ user }}</li>
        {% endfor %}
    </ul>
</body>
</html>
```

Visiting **http://127.0.0.1:5000/users** will display:

- Alice
- Bob
- Charlie

4.3.4 Using Static Files (CSS, JavaScript, Images)

1. **Create a static/ folder** inside your Flask project.
2. **Inside static/, create style.css with the following content:**

css

```
body {
    background-color: #f4f4f4;
```

66

```
font-family: Arial, sans-serif;
}
```

3. Link the CSS in your template (`index.html`)

html

```
<link rel="stylesheet" type="text/css" href="{{
url_for('static', filename='style.css') }}">
```

Now, when you load your page, **the CSS file will be applied!**

Conclusion

In this chapter, you learned:
How Flask's minimalistic architecture works
How to create routes and handle requests
How to use Jinja2 templates for dynamic HTML
How to include static files like CSS and JavaScript

In the next chapter, we'll dive into **handling forms and user input in Flask!**

CHAPTER 5

HANDLING FORMS AND USER INPUT IN FLASK

Forms are essential in web applications for gathering user input, whether it's a **login form, registration form, search bar, or contact form**. Flask provides tools to handle form data securely and efficiently. In this chapter, you'll learn:

How to process form data in Flask
How to use Flask-WTF for form validation
The difference between GET and POST requests in handling user input

---

5.1 Processing Form Data in Flask

In Flask, form data is sent via HTTP **GET** or **POST** requests. The **GET method** appends data in the URL, while the **POST method** sends data in the request body.

5.1.1 Creating a Simple HTML Form

Create an `index.html` file inside the `templates/` folder:

html

```
<!DOCTYPE html>
<html>
<head>
    <title>Flask Form</title>
</head>
<body>
    <h2>Enter Your Name</h2>
    <form action="/submit" method="POST">
        <label for="name">Name:</label>
        <input type="text" name="name" required>
        <button type="submit">Submit</button>
    </form>
</body>
</html>
```

5.1.2 Handling Form Submission in Flask

Modify `app.py` to process form input:

python

```
from flask import Flask, request, render_template

app = Flask(__name__)
```

```python
@app.route("/")
def index():
    return render_template("index.html")


@app.route("/submit", methods=["POST"])
def submit():
    name = request.form["name"]   # Get input value
    return f"Hello, {name}!"


if __name__ == "__main__":
    app.run(debug=True)
```

Explanation:

- **request.form["name"]** retrieves the input value.
- The submitted name is displayed as part of the response.

Run the App:

sh

```
python app.py
```

- Open **http://127.0.0.1:5000/**
- Enter a name and click submit.
- You'll see **"Hello, [Your Name]!"**

5.2 Using Flask-WTF for Form Validation

Flask-WTF simplifies form handling and validation by integrating **WTForms** with Flask.

5.2.1 Installing Flask-WTF

Run:

```sh
pip install flask-wtf
```

5.2.2 Creating a Form with Flask-WTF

Modify `app.py` to include form validation:

```python
from flask import Flask, render_template, request
from flask_wtf import FlaskForm
from wtforms import StringField, SubmitField
from wtforms.validators import DataRequired

app = Flask(__name__)
app.config["SECRET_KEY"] = "mysecretkey"

class NameForm(FlaskForm):
```

71

```
    name  =  StringField("Enter  your  name:",
validators=[DataRequired()])
    submit = SubmitField("Submit")


@app.route("/", methods=["GET", "POST"])
def index():
    form = NameForm()
    if form.validate_on_submit():
        name = form.name.data
        return f"Hello, {name}!"
    return         render_template("form.html",
form=form)


if __name__ == "__main__":
    app.run(debug=True)
```

5.2.3 Creating the `form.html` Template

Inside the `templates/` folder, create `form.html`:

html

```
<!DOCTYPE html>
<html>
<head>
    <title>Flask-WTF Form</title>
</head>
<body>
```

```
<h2>Enter Your Name</h2>
<form method="POST">
      {{ form.hidden_tag() }}
      <p>{{ form.name.label }} {{ form.name()
}}</p>
      <p>{{ form.submit() }}</p>
   </form>
</body>
</html>
```

Explanation:

- **form.hidden_tag()** adds CSRF protection.
- **Flask-WTF handles input validation** and **displays errors automatically**.
- If you try submitting without entering a name, Flask-WTF will show an error.

5.3 Handling GET vs. POST Requests

5.3.1 Understanding GET vs. POST

Method	Description	When to Use
GET	Sends data in the URL	When retrieving data (e.g., search, pagination)

Method	Description	When to Use
POST	Sends data in the request body	When submitting forms securely (e.g., login, registration)

5.3.2 Example: Handling Both GET and POST Requests

Modify app.py to process both **GET** and **POST**:

python

```python
@app.route("/greet", methods=["GET", "POST"])
def greet():
    if request.method == "POST":
        name = request.form["name"]
        return f"Hello, {name}!"
    return '''
        <form method="POST">
            Name:        <input        type="text"
name="name">
            <button
type="submit">Submit</button>
        </form>
    '''
```

How it Works:

- If accessed via **GET**, the form is displayed.
- If submitted via **POST**, it greets the user.

5.3.3 Example: Using GET to Pass Data

Modify `app.py` to use **query parameters**:

python

```
@app.route("/hello")
def hello():
    name = request.args.get("name", "Guest")   #
Get name from URL
    return f"Hello, {name}!"
```

Usage:

- Open **http://127.0.0.1:5000/hello?name=Alex**
- You'll see **"Hello, Alex!"**

GET is useful for search queries, filters, and passing non-sensitive data.

Conclusion

In this chapter, you learned:
How to process form data in Flask
Using Flask-WTF for form validation
Handling GET vs. POST requests

Now that you can handle user input, in the next chapter, we'll explore **Flask and databases using SQLAlchemy**!

CHAPTER 6

FLASK AND DATABASES – SQLALCHEMY

A web application often needs to store and manage data, such as **user information, blog posts, or product listings**. Flask doesn't come with a built-in database system, but it integrates well with **SQLAlchemy**, a powerful Object-Relational Mapping (ORM) library.

In   this   chapter,   you'll   learn:
What SQLAlchemy ORM is and why it's useful
How to connect Flask with SQLite, PostgreSQL, and MySQL
Performing CRUD (Create, Read, Update, Delete) operations using SQLAlchemy

---

6.1 Introduction to SQLAlchemy ORM

What is SQLAlchemy?

SQLAlchemy is a **Python library** that simplifies database interactions by allowing developers to use **Python classes instead of raw SQL queries**.

Eliminates complex SQL queries
Provides a structured way to interact with databases
Works with multiple databases (SQLite, PostgreSQL, MySQL, etc.)

Installing SQLAlchemy

To install SQLAlchemy and Flask-SQLAlchemy, run:

sh

```
pip install flask-sqlalchemy
```

6.2 Connecting Flask with Databases

Flask-SQLAlchemy supports **SQLite, PostgreSQL, MySQL, and other databases**.

6.2.1 Connecting Flask with SQLite (Default for Small Apps)

SQLite is a lightweight, file-based database. To connect, modify app.py:

```
python
```

```python
from flask import Flask
from flask_sqlalchemy import SQLAlchemy

app = Flask(__name__)
app.config["SQLALCHEMY_DATABASE_URI"]          =
"sqlite:///mydatabase.db"
app.config["SQLALCHEMY_TRACK_MODIFICATIONS"]   =
False

db = SQLAlchemy(app)
```

When you run this app, SQLite will create mydatabase.db automatically.

6.2.2 Connecting Flask with PostgreSQL

For PostgreSQL, install psycopg2:

```
sh
```

```
pip install psycopg2
```

Modify `app.py`:

```python
```

```python
app.config["SQLALCHEMY_DATABASE_URI"]          =
"postgresql://username:password@localhost/mydat
abase"
```

6.2.3 Connecting Flask with MySQL

For MySQL, install `mysqlclient`:

```sh
```

```sh
pip install mysqlclient
```

Modify `app.py`:

```python
```

```python
app.config["SQLALCHEMY_DATABASE_URI"]          =
"mysql://username:password@localhost/mydatabase
"
```

Replace `username`, `password`, and `mydatabase` with your actual credentials.

6.3 CRUD Operations with SQLAlchemy

6.3.1 Creating a Model (Table)

A model represents a **table** in the database. Example: **User model** with id, name, and email.

Modify app.py:

python

```python
class User(db.Model):
    id = db.Column(db.Integer, primary_key=True)
    name        =        db.Column(db.String(100),
nullable=False)
    email       =        db.Column(db.String(100),
unique=True, nullable=False)

    def __repr__(self):
        return f"<User {self.name}>"
```

This defines a **User** table with **id, name,** and **email columns.**

6.3.2 Creating the Database

81

Run these commands in **Python shell**:

```sh
sh
```

```python
python
python
```

```
from app import db
db.create_all()
```

This creates the users table in the database.

6.3.3 Inserting Data (Create)

To **add a user**, modify app.py:

```python
python
```

```
@app.route("/add")
def add_user():
    new_user           =           User(name="Alice",
email="alice@example.com")
    db.session.add(new_user)
    db.session.commit()
    return "User added!"
```

Run the server and visit **http://127.0.0.1:5000/add**.

A new user will be stored in the database.

6.3.4 Retrieving Data (Read)

To **fetch all users**:

python

```
@app.route("/users")
def get_users():
    users = User.query.all()
    return "<br>".join([f"{user.id}: {user.name}
- {user.email}" for user in users])
```

Visit **http://127.0.0.1:5000/users** to see all users.

6.3.5 Updating Data (Update)

To **update a user's email**:

python

```
@app.route("/update/<int:id>")
def update_user(id):
    user = User.query.get(id)
```

83

```
if user:
    user.email = "newemail@example.com"
    db.session.commit()
    return f"User {id} updated!"
return "User not found!"
```

Visit **http://127.0.0.1:5000/update/1** to update user with ID
1.

6.3.6 Deleting Data (Delete)

To **delete a user**:

python

```
@app.route("/delete/<int:id>")
def delete_user(id):
    user = User.query.get(id)
    if user:
        db.session.delete(user)
        db.session.commit()
        return f"User {id} deleted!"
    return "User not found!"
```

Visit **http://127.0.0.1:5000/delete/1** to delete user with ID
1.

Conclusion

In this chapter, you learned:
What SQLAlchemy ORM is and why it's useful
How to connect Flask with SQLite, PostgreSQL, and MySQL
Performing CRUD operations with SQLAlchemy

In the next chapter, we'll explore **Flask authentication and security best practices!**

CHAPTER 7

FLASK AUTHENTICATION AND SECURITY

Web applications require **authentication and security** mechanisms to protect user data and ensure safe access. Flask provides various tools for handling authentication, from **user login systems to password hashing and token-based authentication**.

In this chapter, you'll learn:
 How to implement user authentication using Flask-Login
 How to securely store passwords using hashing techniques
 How to use OAuth and JWT authentication for secure API access

7.1 User Authentication with Flask-Login

Flask-Login is an extension that simplifies user session management, allowing developers to handle **logins, logouts, and user sessions**.

7.1.1 Installing Flask-Login

Run:

```sh
pip install flask-login
```

7.1.2 Setting Up Flask-Login

Modify app.py:

```python
from flask import Flask, render_template,
redirect, url_for, request
from flask_sqlalchemy import SQLAlchemy
from flask_login import LoginManager, UserMixin,
login_user, login_required, logout_user,
current_user
```

```
app = Flask(__name__)
app.config["SQLALCHEMY_DATABASE_URI"]          =
"sqlite:///users.db"
app.config["SECRET_KEY"] = "mysecretkey"


db = SQLAlchemy(app)
login_manager = LoginManager()
login_manager.init_app(app)
login_manager.login_view = "login"


# User Model
class User(db.Model, UserMixin):
    id = db.Column(db.Integer, primary_key=True)
    username      =      db.Column(db.String(100),
unique=True, nullable=False)
    password      =      db.Column(db.String(100),
nullable=False)


@login_manager.user_loader
def load_user(user_id):
    return User.query.get(int(user_id))
```

What's happening here?

- **UserMixin** simplifies user authentication by providing required attributes.
- **login_manager.user_loader** tells Flask-Login how to load a user.

7.1.3 Creating Login and Logout Routes

Modify `app.py`:

python

```python
from flask_login import login_user, logout_user,
login_required

@app.route("/login", methods=["GET", "POST"])
def login():
    if request.method == "POST":
        username = request.form["username"]
        password = request.form["password"]
        user                                  =
User.query.filter_by(username=username).first()

        if user and user.password == password:  #
(We'll hash this later!)
            login_user(user)
            return
redirect(url_for("dashboard"))

        return "Invalid credentials!"

    return '''
        <form method="POST">
```

89

```
        Username:      <input      type="text"
name="username">
        Password:    <input    type="password"
name="password">
        <button type="submit">Login</button>
    </form>
    '''


@app.route("/logout")
@login_required
def logout():
    logout_user()
    return redirect(url_for("login"))


@app.route("/dashboard")
@login_required
def dashboard():
    return f"Welcome, {current_user.username}!"
```

Important:

- **login_user(user)** starts a session.
- **login_required** ensures only logged-in users can access pages.
- **logout_user()** logs the user out.

7.2 Password Hashing and Security Best Practices

Storing passwords as plain text is a **major security risk**. Instead, we use **password hashing** to securely store user passwords.

7.2.1 Installing Flask-Bcrypt

Run:

```sh
```

```sh
pip install flask-bcrypt
```

Modify app.py:

```python
```

```python
from flask_bcrypt import Bcrypt

bcrypt = Bcrypt(app)

# Updating User Registration to Store Hashed
Passwords
@app.route("/register", methods=["GET", "POST"])
def register():
    if request.method == "POST":
        username = request.form["username"]
```

```
        hashed_password                        =
bcrypt.generate_password_hash(request.form["pas
sword"]).decode("utf-8")
        new_user    =    User(username=username,
password=hashed_password)

        db.session.add(new_user)
        db.session.commit()
        return "User registered successfully!"

    return '''
        <form method="POST">
            Username:    <input    type="text"
name="username">
            Password:    <input    type="password"
name="password">
            <button
type="submit">Register</button>
        </form>
    '''
```

7.2.2 Updating Login to Use Hashed Passwords

Modify `login()` function:

```
python
```

```
if                    user                    and
bcrypt.check_password_hash(user.password,
password):
    login_user(user)
    return redirect(url_for("dashboard"))
```

Now, passwords are securely stored and compared using hashing!

7.3 Implementing OAuth and JWT Authentication

7.3.1 OAuth Authentication with Flask-Dance

OAuth allows users to log in with third-party providers like **Google, Facebook, or GitHub**.

Step 1: Install Flask-Dance

sh

```
pip install flask-dance
```

Step 2: Setup Google OAuth

Modify app.py:

python

```
from       flask_dance.contrib.google      import
make_google_blueprint, google

google_bp                                        =
make_google_blueprint(client_id="YOUR_CLIENT_ID
",

client_secret="YOUR_CLIENT_SECRET",

redirect_to="google_login")

app.register_blueprint(google_bp,
url_prefix="/login")

@app.route("/google")
def google_login():
    if not google.authorized:
        return redirect(url_for("google.login"))
    resp = google.get("/userinfo")
    return f"Hello, {resp.json()['name']}!"
```

Now users can log in with Google!

7.3.2 Implementing JWT Authentication (For APIs)

JWT (JSON Web Token) is a secure way to handle authentication in **Flask APIs**.

Step 1: Install Flask-JWT-Extended

sh

```
pip install flask-jwt-extended
```

Step 2: Configure JWT in app.py

python

```
from flask_jwt_extended import JWTManager,
create_access_token, jwt_required,
get_jwt_identity

app.config["JWT_SECRET_KEY"] = "supersecretkey"
jwt = JWTManager(app)
```

Step 3: Generate JWT Token on Login

Modify login() function:

python

```
@app.route("/token", methods=["POST"])
def token():
    username = request.json.get("username")
    password = request.json.get("password")
    user =
User.query.filter_by(username=username).first()
```

95

```
    if                user                and
bcrypt.check_password_hash(user.password,
password):
        access_token                      =
create_access_token(identity=user.id)
        return {"access_token": access_token}

    return {"message": "Invalid credentials"},
401
```

Step 4: Protect Routes with JWT

```python
@app.route("/protected", methods=["GET"])
@jwt_required()
def protected():
    user_id = get_jwt_identity()
    return {"message": f"User {user_id} has
access!"}
```

Now, API users must send a valid JWT token to access `/protected`!

Conclusion

In this chapter, you learned:
How to handle user authentication using Flask-Login
How to securely store passwords using Flask-Bcrypt

How to implement OAuth authentication with Flask-Dance

How to secure APIs using JWT authentication

Next, we'll dive into **Flask API development and building RESTful services!**

CHAPTER 8

FLASK API DEVELOPMENT – BUILDING RESTFUL SERVICES

APIs (Application Programming Interfaces) allow web applications to **communicate** with each other. **Flask** makes it easy to build **RESTful APIs**, which follow REST (Representational State Transfer) principles to enable efficient data exchange.

In this chapter, you'll learn:
How to create APIs with Flask
Using Flask-RESTful and Flask-SQLAlchemy for structured API development
Returning JSON responses and handling API errors properly

8.1 Creating APIs with Flask

A **REST API** enables CRUD (Create, Read, Update, Delete) operations using HTTP methods:

HTTP Method Operation

GET   Retrieve data

POST   Create new data

PUT   Update existing data

DELETE   Remove data

8.1.1 Installing Flask-RESTful

Flask-RESTful is an extension that helps create structured APIs.

Install it:

```sh
sh
```

```sh
pip install flask-restful
```

8.1.2 Setting Up a Simple API

Modify app.py:

```python
python
```

```
from flask import Flask, jsonify
from flask_restful import Api, Resource

app = Flask(__name__)
api = Api(app)

class HelloWorld(Resource):
    def get(self):
        return jsonify({"message": "Hello, Flask
API!"})

api.add_resource(HelloWorld, "/")

if __name__ == "__main__":
    app.run(debug=True)
```

Run the app and visit `http://127.0.0.1:5000/`
You'll get a **JSON response**:

```
json

{"message": "Hello, Flask API!"}
```

8.2 Using Flask-RESTful and Flask-SQLAlchemy

Now, let's **connect the API to a database** using **Flask-SQLAlchemy**.

100

8.2.1 Setting Up the Database

Modify `app.py`:

python

```
from flask_sqlalchemy import SQLAlchemy

app.config["SQLALCHEMY_DATABASE_URI"]           =
"sqlite:///books.db"
db = SQLAlchemy(app)
```

This connects the API to a **SQLite database**.

8.2.2 Creating a Database Model

Define a **Book model** in `app.py`:

python

```
class Book(db.Model):
    id = db.Column(db.Integer, primary_key=True)
    title       =        db.Column(db.String(100),
nullable=False)
```

```
    author         =         db.Column(db.String(100),
nullable=False)

    def to_dict(self):
        return    {"id":    self.id,    "title":
self.title, "author": self.author}
```

The **to_dict()** method converts database records into a JSON-friendly format.

Run these commands in Python shell:

```sh
sh
```

```
python
python
```

```
from app import db
db.create_all()
```

This creates the **books.db** database.

8.3 Implementing CRUD Operations in the API

Now, let's add API endpoints to **create, read, update, and delete books**.

8.3.1 Retrieving All Books (GET Request)

Modify app.py:

python

```python
class BookList(Resource):
    def get(self):
        books = Book.query.all()
        return jsonify([book.to_dict() for book
in books])


api.add_resource(BookList, "/books")
```

Visit   **http://127.0.0.1:5000/books**
Response (if books exist):

json

```json
[
  {"id": 1, "title": "1984", "author": "George
Orwell"},
  {"id":  2,  "title":  "The  Great  Gatsby",
"author": "F. Scott Fitzgerald"}
]
```

8.3.2 Retrieving a Single Book (GET Request)

python

```python
class BookDetail(Resource):
    def get(self, book_id):
        book = Book.query.get(book_id)
        if book:
            return jsonify(book.to_dict())
        return jsonify({"error": "Book not
found"}), 404

api.add_resource(BookDetail,
"/books/<int:book_id>")
```

Visit   **http://127.0.0.1:5000/books/1**
Response:

json

```json
{"id": 1, "title": "1984", "author": "George
Orwell"}
```

8.3.3 Adding a New Book (POST Request)

Modify app.py:

python

```
from flask import request

class AddBook(Resource):
    def post(self):
        data = request.get_json()
        new_book   =   Book(title=data["title"],
author=data["author"])
        db.session.add(new_book)
        db.session.commit()
        return jsonify(new_book.to_dict()), 201

api.add_resource(AddBook, "/books")
```

Send a POST request using Postman or cURL:

sh

```
curl  -X  POST  "http://127.0.0.1:5000/books"  -H
"Content-Type:  application/json"  -d  '{"title":
"New Book", "author": "Author Name"}'
```

Response:

json

```
{"id": 3, "title": "New Book", "author": "Author
Name"}
```

8.3.4 Updating a Book (PUT Request)

python

```python
class UpdateBook(Resource):
    def put(self, book_id):
        book = Book.query.get(book_id)
        if book:
            data = request.get_json()
            book.title    =    data.get("title",
book.title)
            book.author    =    data.get("author",
book.author)
            db.session.commit()
            return jsonify(book.to_dict())
        return    jsonify({"error":    "Book    not
found"}), 404


api.add_resource(UpdateBook,
"/books/<int:book_id>")
```

Send a PUT request:

sh

```sh
curl -X PUT "http://127.0.0.1:5000/books/3" -H
"Content-Type: application/json" -d '{"title":
"Updated Book"}'
```

Response:

```
json
```

```
{"id": 3, "title": "Updated Book", "author":
"Author Name"}
```

8.3.5 Deleting a Book (DELETE Request)

```python
class DeleteBook(Resource):
    def delete(self, book_id):
        book = Book.query.get(book_id)
        if book:
            db.session.delete(book)
            db.session.commit()
            return jsonify({"message": "Book
deleted"})
        return jsonify({"error": "Book not
found"}), 404


api.add_resource(DeleteBook,
"/books/<int:book_id>")
```

Send a DELETE request:

```sh
sh
```

```
curl -X DELETE "http://127.0.0.1:5000/books/3"
```

Response:

```
json
```

```
{"message": "Book deleted"}
```

8.4 Handling API Errors

Flask-RESTful allows better error handling.

Modify `app.py`:

```python
python
```

```python
from werkzeug.exceptions import HTTPException

@app.errorhandler(HTTPException)
def handle_exception(e):
    return jsonify({"error": e.name, "message":
e.description}), e.code


@app.errorhandler(404)
def not_found_error(error):
    return    jsonify({"error":    "Not    Found",
"message":  "The  requested  resource  was  not
found"}), 404
```

```
@app.errorhandler(500)
def internal_error(error):
    return jsonify({"error": "Internal Server
Error", "message": "An unexpected error
occurred"}), 500
```

Now, Flask will return JSON-formatted error messages.

Conclusion

In this chapter, you learned:
**How to create REST APIs with Flask-RESTful
Connecting APIs to a database with Flask-SQLAlchemy
Performing CRUD operations with API endpoints
Handling API errors effectively**

Next, we'll explore **Flask and security best practices!**

CHAPTER 9

DEPLOYING FLASK APPS

Developing a Flask application is just the first step—**deploying it to a live server** ensures that users can access your application from anywhere. Deployment requires configuring servers, setting up a production environment, and optimizing performance.

In this chapter, you'll learn:
How to deploy Flask applications on Heroku and AWS
How to configure Gunicorn and Nginx for production
How to containerize Flask applications using Docker

9.1 Hosting Flask Applications on Heroku and AWS

9.1.1 Deploying Flask on Heroku

Step 1: Install Heroku CLI

Download and install the Heroku CLI from Heroku's official website.

Step 2: Prepare Your Flask Project

Your project should have:
`app.py` (Main Flask app)
`requirements.txt` (List of dependencies)
`Procfile` (Defines how to run the app)

To create `requirements.txt`:

sh

```
pip freeze > requirements.txt
```

Create a `Procfile` with the following content:

makefile

```
web: gunicorn app:app
```

Gunicorn is a production WSGI server.

Step 3: Initialize a Git Repository
sh

```
git init
git add .
git commit -m "Initial commit"
```

Step 4: Deploy to Heroku

1. Login to Heroku:

   sh

   heroku login

2. Create a new Heroku app:

   sh

   heroku create flask-app-demo

3. Deploy the code:

   sh

   git push heroku main

4. Open the deployed app:

   sh

   heroku open

Your Flask app is now live on Heroku!

9.1.2 Deploying Flask on AWS EC2

Step 1: Launch an EC2 Instance

1. Go to **AWS EC2 Console**
2. Choose **Ubuntu** as the operating system
3. Configure the security group to allow HTTP (port 80)

Step 2: Connect to the EC2 Instance

Run:

```sh
```

```sh
ssh -i "your-key.pem" ubuntu@your-ec2-ip
```

Step 3: Install Dependencies

On the EC2 instance:

```sh
```

```sh
sudo apt update
sudo apt install python3-pip python3-venv
```

Step 4: Clone Your Flask App

```sh
```

```sh
git clone https://github.com/your-repo/flask-app.git
cd flask-app
```

113

```
python3 -m venv venv
source venv/bin/activate
pip install -r requirements.txt
```

Step 5: Run Flask with Gunicorn

sh

```
gunicorn -w 4 -b 0.0.0.0:5000 app:app
```

Your Flask app is running on AWS EC2!

9.2 Configuring Gunicorn and Nginx

Gunicorn handles requests efficiently, while **Nginx** acts as a reverse proxy to route traffic.

9.2.1 Installing Gunicorn and Running Flask

Install Gunicorn:

sh

```
pip install gunicorn
```

Run your Flask app with Gunicorn:

sh

```
gunicorn -w 4 -b 0.0.0.0:8000 app:app
```

9.2.2 Installing and Configuring Nginx

On an Ubuntu server, install Nginx:

sh

```
sudo apt install nginx
```

Create a configuration file for Nginx:

sh

```
sudo nano /etc/nginx/sites-available/flask_app
```

Add the following:

nginx

```
server {
    listen 80;
    server_name your-domain.com;

    location / {
        proxy_pass http://127.0.0.1:8000;
        proxy_set_header Host $host;
        proxy_set_header X-Real-IP $remote_addr;
    }
```

}

Activate the configuration:

sh

```
sudo ln -s /etc/nginx/sites-available/flask_app
/etc/nginx/sites-enabled
sudo systemctl restart nginx
```

Now, Nginx will forward requests to your Flask app!

9.3 Using Docker to Containerize Flask Apps

Docker helps package applications into **containers** that run consistently across different environments.

9.3.1 Installing Docker

On Ubuntu, install Docker:

sh

```
sudo apt update
sudo apt install docker.io
```

Verify installation:

```sh
docker --version
```

9.3.2 Writing a Dockerfile

Create a `Dockerfile` in your Flask project:

```dockerfile
# Use an official Python image
FROM python:3.9

# Set the working directory
WORKDIR /app

#  project files
 . /app

# Install dependencies
RUN pip install -r requirements.txt

# Expose the application port
EXPOSE 5000

# Command to run Flask app
CMD ["gunicorn", "-w", "4", "-b", "0.0.0.0:5000", "app:app"]
```

9.3.3 Building and Running a Docker Container

Build the Docker image:

```sh
docker build -t flask-app .
```

Run the container:

```sh
docker run -p 5000:5000 flask-app
```

Your Flask app is now running inside a Docker container!

9.3.4 Deploying a Dockerized Flask App

You can deploy your Docker container to **Docker Hub** or **AWS ECS**.

1. **Tag the Image:**

```sh
```

```
docker    tag    flask-app    your-dockerhub-
username/flask-app
```

2. **Push to Docker Hub:**

```sh
```

```
docker push your-dockerhub-username/flask-
app
```

3. **Run on a Remote Server:**

```sh
```

```
docker pull your-dockerhub-username/flask-
app
docker run -p 5000:5000 your-dockerhub-
username/flask-app
```

Your Dockerized Flask app is now deployed!

Conclusion

In   this   chapter,   you   learned:
How to deploy Flask apps on Heroku and AWS

How to configure Gunicorn and Nginx for production

How to containerize Flask apps using Docker

Next, we'll explore **Flask middleware and security best practices!**

CHAPTER 10

DJANGO FUNDAMENTALS – PROJECT SETUP AND MVT ARCHITECTURE

Django is a **full-stack framework** that follows the **Model-View-Template (MVT) architecture**, making it one of the most powerful tools for web development. It simplifies handling databases, managing URLs, and rendering HTML templates.

In this chapter, you'll learn:
How to set up Django and understand the MVT pattern
How to manage Django applications using `manage.py`
How to create your first Django views and templates

10.1 Setting Up Django and Understanding the MVT Architecture

10.1.1 Installing Django

121

Make sure you have Python installed, then install Django:

sh

```
pip install django
```

Verify the installation:

sh

```
django-admin --version
```

10.1.2 Creating a Django Project

To start a Django project, run:

sh

```
django-admin startproject myproject
cd myproject
```

This creates the following structure:

csharp

```
myproject/
|— manage.py          # Django's command-line
tool
|— myproject/         # Main project folder
```

122

```
|     |— __init__.py      # Marks it as a package
|     |— settings.py      # Project settings
|     |— urls.py          # URL routing
|     |— wsgi.py          # WSGI server entry point
```

10.1.3 Understanding Django's MVT Architecture

Django follows the **Model-View-Template (MVT) pattern**, which separates **data, business logic, and presentation**.

Component   Role

Model (M)   Defines database structure

View (V)   Handles business logic and data processing

Template (T) Controls how data is presented to users

10.2 Managing Apps with Django's manage.py

Django projects are structured into **apps** that handle specific functionalities.

10.2.1 Creating an App

Run:

```sh
python manage.py startapp myapp
```

This creates:

```php
myapp/
|— models.py          # Defines database models
|— views.py           # Handles application logic
|— templates/         # Stores HTML templates
|— static/            # Stores CSS/JS files
|— urls.py           # Defines app-specific routes
|— admin.py            # Manages Django's admin
interface
```

Each app is modular and reusable!

10.2.2 Running the Django Development Server

Run:

```sh
python manage.py runserver
```

Output:

```
nginx
```

```
Starting        development        server        at
http://127.0.0.1:8000/
```

Open **http://127.0.0.1:8000/** to see Django's default welcome page.

10.3 First Django Views and Templates

10.3.1 Creating a Simple View

Modify myapp/views.py:

```python
python

from django.http import HttpResponse

def home(request):
    return HttpResponse("Hello, Django!")
```

10.3.2 Connecting the View to a URL

Modify myproject/urls.py:

```
python
```

```
from django.contrib import admin
from django.urls import path
from myapp.views import home

urlpatterns = [
    path('admin/', admin.site.urls),
    path('', home),
]
```

Visit `http://127.0.0.1:8000/` to see "Hello, Django!".

10.3.3 Using Templates for Dynamic Content

Step 1: Create a `templates` Folder

Inside `myapp/`, **create:**

```
arduino
```

```
myapp/
└── templates/
    └── home.html
```

Step 2: Create home.html

Edit myapp/templates/home.html:

html

```
<!DOCTYPE html>
<html>
<head>
    <title>Django App</title>
</head>
<body>
    <h1>Welcome, {{ name }}!</h1>
</body>
</html>
```

Step 3: Modify views.py *to Use Templates*

python

```
from django.shortcuts import render

def home(request):
    return render(request, "home.html", {"name":
"Django Developer"})
```

Now, Django will render home.html with dynamic data!

Conclusion

In this chapter, you learned:

How to set up a Django project and understand MVT architecture

How to manage Django apps using `manage.py`

How to create Django views and templates

Next, we'll dive into **Django models and databases!**

CHAPTER 11

DJANGO MODELS AND DATABASES

Django comes with **Django ORM (Object-Relational Mapping)**, which allows you to interact with a database using Python instead of writing raw SQL queries. It simplifies database management and makes querying data more efficient.

In this chapter, you'll learn:
How to define models using Django ORM
How to perform database migrations
How to query data efficiently using Django's QuerySet API

11.1 Defining Models with Django ORM

A **model** in Django defines the structure of database tables. Instead of writing SQL commands, you use Python classes that Django automatically translates into database tables.

11.1.1 Creating a Model

Modify `myapp/models.py`:

python

```python
from django.db import models

class Book(models.Model):
    title = models.CharField(max_length=200)
    author = models.CharField(max_length=100)
    published_date = models.DateField()
    isbn    =    models.CharField(max_length=13,
unique=True)

    def __str__(self):
        return self.title
```

11.1.2 Understanding Model Fields

Field Type	Purpose
CharField	Stores text (with a max length)
DateField	Stores date values
IntegerField	Stores integer numbers

Field Type   Purpose

`BooleanField` Stores True/False values

`ForeignKey`   Creates relationships between models

The __str__() method returns a readable representation of the object.

11.2 Performing Migrations

Once a model is defined, it needs to be **migrated** to create the actual database table.

11.2.1 Applying Migrations

Run:

```sh
```

```
python manage.py makemigrations myapp
```

This generates a migration file in `migrations/`:

```bash
```

```
Migrations for 'myapp':
  myapp/migrations/0001_initial.py
    - Create model Book
```

Now, apply the migration:

sh

```
python manage.py migrate
```

This creates the books table in the database!

11.3 Querying Data Efficiently

11.3.1 Inserting Data (Create)

Open the **Django shell**:

sh

```
python manage.py shell
```

Add a book to the database:

python

```
from myapp.models import Book
```

```
book    =    Book(title="Django    for    Beginners",
author="William              S.              Vincent",
published_date="2023-06-10",
isbn="1234567890123")
book.save()
```

This saves the book to the database!

11.3.2 Retrieving Data (Read)

Fetch all books:

```
python
```

```
books = Book.objects.all()
print(books)
```

Fetch a single book:

```
python
```

```
book = Book.objects.get(id=1)
print(book.title)
```

11.3.3 Updating Data (Update)

```python
python

book = Book.objects.get(id=1)
book.title = "Updated Django Guide"
book.save()
```

Now, the book title is updated!

11.3.4 Deleting Data (Delete)

```python
python

book = Book.objects.get(id=1)
book.delete()
```

The book is now deleted from the database!

Conclusion

In this chapter, you learned:
How to define models using Django ORM
How to perform migrations
How to query and manage data efficiently

Next, we'll explore **Django forms and data validation!**

CHAPTER 12

DJANGO FORMS AND MODELFORMS

Forms are an essential part of web applications, allowing users to submit data, interact with databases, and perform actions like user registration, feedback submission, and authentication. Django provides a powerful built-in **forms system** that simplifies data handling and validation.

In this chapter, you'll learn:
How to create forms in Django
How to handle user input securely
How to use Django ModelForms for simplified data validation

12.1 Creating Forms in Django

Django provides a `forms` **module** to handle form creation, data processing, and validation. Instead of manually writing HTML forms and processing inputs, Django automates this process.

12.1.1 Creating a Basic Form

Modify myapp/forms.py:

python

```python
from django import forms

class ContactForm(forms.Form):
    name = forms.CharField(max_length=100)
    email = forms.EmailField()
    message                                 =
forms.CharField(widget=forms.Textarea)
```

This form includes three fields:

- name: A text input with a max length of 100
- email: An email input that ensures valid email addresses
- message: A larger text area for messages

12.1.2 Rendering Forms in a Template

Modify myapp/views.py:

python

```python
from django.shortcuts import render
```

```
from .forms import ContactForm

def contact(request):
    form = ContactForm()
    return    render(request,    "contact.html",
{"form": form})
```

Create templates/contact.html:

html

```
<!DOCTYPE html>
<html>
<head>
    <title>Contact Form</title>
</head>
<body>
    <h2>Contact Us</h2>
    <form method="POST">
        {% csrf_token %}
        {{ form.as_p }}
        <button type="submit">Submit</button>
    </form>
</body>
</html>
```

{{ form.as_p }} renders form fields with <p> tags for better   spacing.

{% csrf_token %} protects against cross-site request forgery (CSRF) attacks.

12.2 Handling User Input

When a user submits the form, Django processes the input data.

Modify myapp/views.py:

python

```python
def contact(request):
    if request.method == "POST":
        form = ContactForm(request.POST)
        if form.is_valid():
            name = form.cleaned_data["name"]
            email = form.cleaned_data["email"]
            message                              =
form.cleaned_data["message"]
            return                  render(request,
"success.html", {"name": name})
    else:
        form = ContactForm()
    return      render(request,      "contact.html",
{"form": form})
```

Key Methods:

- **is_valid()**: Checks if form data meets validation criteria
- **cleaned_data**: Retrieves cleaned user input

12.3 Using Django ModelForms for Easy Data Validation

Instead of manually defining form fields, **ModelForms** auto-generate forms based on Django models.

12.3.1 Creating a ModelForm

Modify myapp/forms.py:

python

```python
from django.forms import ModelForm
from .models import Book

class BookForm(ModelForm):
    class Meta:
        model = Book
        fields    =    ["title",    "author",
"published_date", "isbn"]
```

This ModelForm automatically generates form fields based on the `Book` model.

12.3.2 Using ModelForm in a View

Modify `myapp/views.py`:

python

```python
from django.shortcuts import render, redirect
from .forms import BookForm

def add_book(request):
    if request.method == "POST":
        form = BookForm(request.POST)
        if form.is_valid():
            form.save()
            return redirect("success")
    else:
        form = BookForm()
    return render(request, "add_book.html", {"form": form})
```

12.3.3 Rendering ModelForm in a Template

Create `templates/add_book.html`:

html

```
<!DOCTYPE html>
<html>
<head>
    <title>Add a Book</title>
</head>
<body>
    <h2>Add a New Book</h2>
    <form method="POST">
        {% csrf_token %}
        {{ form.as_p }}
        <button type="submit">Add Book</button>
    </form>
</body>
</html>
```

Now, the form automatically saves books to the database!

Conclusion

In this chapter, you learned:

How to create forms in Django

How to handle user input securely

How to use Django ModelForms for quick database interactions

Next, we'll explore **Django's authentication system and user management!**

CHAPTER 13

DJANGO AUTHENTICATION SYSTEM

User authentication is a crucial part of web applications. Django provides a **built-in authentication system** that simplifies handling **user login, logout, password management, and user profiles**.

In this chapter, you'll learn:
How Django's built-in authentication system works
How to implement login, logout, and password reset
How to customize authentication with user profiles

13.1 User Authentication with Django's Built-in System

Django includes a fully-featured authentication system that supports:
User   login/logout
Password   hashing   &   authentication
Password   reset   via   email
Custom user profiles

143

13.1.1 Setting Up Django Authentication

Django provides a built-in `User` model that can be used for authentication. Before using it, ensure `django.contrib.auth` is enabled in `settings.py`:

python

```python
INSTALLED_APPS = [
    'django.contrib.auth',
    'django.contrib.contenttypes',
    'django.contrib.sessions',
    'django.contrib.messages',
    'django.contrib.admin',
]
```

Django automatically manages users via the built-in `User` model.

13.1.2 Creating and Managing Users

You can create a superuser for admin access:

sh

```sh
python manage.py createsuperuser
```

Enter details (username, email, password), then log in at `http://127.0.0.1:8000/admin/`.

Now, Django's authentication system is ready to use!

13.2 Implementing Login, Logout, and Password Reset

13.2.1 Implementing User Login

Modify `myapp/views.py`:

python

```
from django.shortcuts import render, redirect
from django.contrib.auth import authenticate,
login

def user_login(request):
    if request.method == "POST":
        username = request.POST["username"]
        password = request.POST["password"]
        user      =         authenticate(request,
username=username, password=password)
        if user is not None:
            login(request, user)
            return redirect("dashboard")
        else:
```

```
        return render(request, "login.html",
{"error": "Invalid credentials"})
    return render(request, "login.html")
```

Create templates/login.html:

html

```html
<!DOCTYPE html>
<html>
<head>
    <title>Login</title>
</head>
<body>
    <h2>Login</h2>
    {% if error %}<p style="color:red;">{{ error
}}</p>{% endif %}
    <form method="POST">
        {% csrf_token %}
        <label>Username:</label>        <input
type="text" name="username" required><br>
        <label>Password:</label>        <input
type="password" name="password" required><br>
        <button type="submit">Login</button>
    </form>
</body>
</html>
```

146

Now users can log in using Django's authentication system!

13.2.2 Implementing Logout

Modify `myapp/views.py`:

```python
python
```

```python
from django.contrib.auth import logout

def user_logout(request):
    logout(request)
    return redirect("login")
```

Add a logout button to `dashboard.html`:

```html
html
```

```html
<a href="{% url 'logout' %}">Logout</a>
```

Users are now logged out when clicking the link!

13.2.3 Implementing Password Reset

Django provides built-in views for password reset. Add this to `urls.py`:

python

```python
from django.contrib.auth import views as auth_views

urlpatterns = [
    path('password_reset/',
auth_views.PasswordResetView.as_view(),
name='password_reset'),
    path('password_reset/done/',
auth_views.PasswordResetDoneView.as_view(),
name='password_reset_done'),
    path('reset/<uidb64>/<token>/',
auth_views.PasswordResetConfirmView.as_view(),
name='password_reset_confirm'),
    path('reset/done/',
auth_views.PasswordResetCompleteView.as_view(),
name='password_reset_complete'),
]
```

Now Django will handle password reset via email!

13.3 Customizing Authentication with User Profiles

13.3.1 Extending Django's User Model

To store extra user data (e.g., profile pictures, bio), create a UserProfile model.

Modify myapp/models.py:

python

```
from django.contrib.auth.models import User
from django.db import models

class UserProfile(models.Model):
    user       =        models.OneToOneField(User,
on_delete=models.CASCADE)
    bio = models.TextField(blank=True)
    profile_picture                          =
models.ImageField(upload_to="profile_pics/",
blank=True)

    def __str__(self):
        return self.user.username
```

Each user now has an associated profile.

13.3.2 Automatically Creating Profiles

Modify `myapp/signals.py`:

```python
from django.db.models.signals import post_save
from django.dispatch import receiver
from .models import UserProfile
from django.contrib.auth.models import User

@receiver(post_save, sender=User)
def create_profile(sender, instance, created, **kwargs):
    if created:

UserProfile.objects.create(user=instance)
```

Modify `apps.py` to register signals:

```python
def ready(self):
    import myapp.signals
```

Now, a profile is created every time a new user registers!

13.3.3 Displaying User Profiles

Modify `myapp/views.py`:

python

```
from    django.contrib.auth.decorators    import
login_required
from .models import UserProfile

@login_required
def profile(request):
    profile                              =
UserProfile.objects.get(user=request.user)
    return    render(request,    "profile.html",
{"profile": profile})
```

Create `templates/profile.html`:

html

```
<!DOCTYPE html>
<html>
<head>
    <title>User Profile</title>
</head>
<body>
    <h2>Welcome,    {{    profile.user.username
}}!</h2>
```

```
    <p>Bio: {{ profile.bio }}</p>
    {% if profile.profile_picture %}
        <img src="{{ profile.profile_picture.url
}}" width="100">
    {% endif %}
</body>
</html>
```

Now users can view their profile information!

Conclusion

In this chapter, you learned:
How to use Django's built-in authentication system
How to implement login, logout, and password reset
How to customize authentication with user profiles

Next, we'll explore **Django's admin panel and how to customize it!**

CHAPTER 14

DJANGO ADMIN PANEL AND CUSTOMIZATION

Django comes with a **built-in admin panel** that provides a powerful interface for managing database records, users, and permissions. It allows developers to quickly add, update, and delete records without writing SQL queries.

In this chapter, you'll learn:

How to use the Django admin panel

How to customize the admin interface

How to create superuser roles and manage permissions

14.1 Understanding the Django Admin Panel

14.1.1 Enabling the Django Admin Panel

The admin panel is enabled by default in Django. Ensure it is listed in INSTALLED_APPS in settings.py:

```python
python
```

```
INSTALLED_APPS = [
    'django.contrib.admin',
    'django.contrib.auth',
    'django.contrib.contenttypes',
    'django.contrib.sessions',
    'django.contrib.messages',
    'django.contrib.staticfiles',
]
```

14.1.2 Running the Admin Panel

1. **Run migrations** to set up the admin panel database tables:

   sh

   ```
   python manage.py migrate
   ```

2. **Create a superuser** to access the admin panel:

   sh

   ```
   python manage.py createsuperuser
   ```

   Enter details (username, email, password).

3. **Start the server**:

   sh

```
python manage.py runserver
```

4. **Access the admin panel**: Open **http://127.0.0.1:8000/admin/** and log in with your superuser credentials.

You should now see the Django admin dashboard!

14.2 Customizing the Admin Interface

By default, Django's admin panel displays only the `User` model. Let's register our own models and customize their appearance.

14.2.1 Registering Models in Admin

Modify `myapp/admin.py`:

```python

from django.contrib import admin
from .models import Book

admin.site.register(Book)
```

Now, the `Book` model will appear in the admin panel!

14.2.2 Customizing the Admin Panel

Django allows customization of how models appear in the admin panel.

Modify `admin.py`:

```python
```

```python
class BookAdmin(admin.ModelAdmin):
    list_display   =    ("title",    "author",
"published_date")
    search_fields = ("title", "author")
    list_filter = ("published_date",)

admin.site.register(Book, BookAdmin)
```

Now, the admin panel will include search functionality and filters!

Visit `/admin/` and see the improved Book management interface!

14.3 Creating Superuser Roles and Permissions

14.3.1 Adding Permissions to Users

Django has built-in **permissions** that allow users to:

- **View** (`view_modelname`)
- **Add** (`add_modelname`)
- **Change** (`change_modelname`)
- **Delete** (`delete_modelname`)

To assign permissions via the admin panel:

1. Navigate to **Users** in the admin panel
2. Select a user
3. Under **Permissions**, assign required access

Now, users will have restricted access based on their assigned permissions!

14.3.2 Creating a Staff User

If you want someone to manage content but **not access everything**, create a **staff user**:

```sh
sh
```

```
python manage.py createsuperuser --username
staff --email staff@example.com
```

Then modify `admin.py` to allow staff users to edit only specific models:

```python
python
```

```
class BookAdmin(admin.ModelAdmin):
    def has_delete_permission(self, request,
obj=None):
        return request.user.is_superuser  # Only
superusers can delete

admin.site.register(Book, BookAdmin)
```

Now, staff users can edit but not delete records!

Conclusion

In this chapter, you learned:
How to use the Django admin panel
How to customize the admin interface
How to create superusers and manage permissions

Next, we'll explore **Django REST Framework (DRF) for building APIs!**

CHAPTER 15

DJANGO REST FRAMEWORK (DRF) FOR APIS

Django REST Framework (DRF) is a **powerful toolkit** for building APIs with Django. It extends Django's functionality to provide tools for creating **RESTful APIs**, handling serialization, authentication, and permissions with ease.

In this chapter, you'll learn:
How Django REST Framework works
How to use serializers and views in DRF
How to implement authentication and permissions in APIs

15.1 Introduction to Django REST Framework

15.1.1 Why Use Django REST Framework?

Django REST Framework (DRF) simplifies API development by providing:

Automatic serialization of Django models
Built-in authentication (Token, JWT, OAuth, etc.)
Browsable API for testing

15.1.2 Installing Django REST Framework

Run:

```sh
```

```sh
pip install djangorestframework
```

Add it to `INSTALLED_APPS` in `settings.py`:

```python
```

```python
INSTALLED_APPS = [
    'rest_framework',
]
```

DRF is now ready to use!

15.2 Serializers and Views in DRF

15.2.1 Creating a Serializer

Serializers convert Django models into **JSON** and vice versa.

Modify `myapp/serializers.py`:

python

```python
from rest_framework import serializers
from .models import Book

class BookSerializer(serializers.ModelSerializer):
    class Meta:
        model = Book
        fields = "__all__"
```

This automatically maps model fields to API data!

15.2.2 Creating API Views

Modify `myapp/views.py`:

python

```python
from rest_framework import generics
from .models import Book
from .serializers import BookSerializer
```

```
class BookList(generics.ListCreateAPIView):
    queryset = Book.objects.all()
    serializer_class = BookSerializer


class
BookDetail(generics.RetrieveUpdateDestroyAPIVie
w):
    queryset = Book.objects.all()
    serializer_class = BookSerializer
```

15.2.3 Adding URLs for APIs

Modify myapp/urls.py:

python

```
from django.urls import path
from .views import BookList, BookDetail

urlpatterns = [
    path("api/books/",        BookList.as_view(),
name="book-list"),
    path("api/books/<int:pk>/",
BookDetail.as_view(), name="book-detail"),
]
```

Your API is now available at /api/books/!

15.3 Authentication and Permissions in DRF

By default, Django REST Framework allows **open access** to APIs. Let's secure them.

15.3.1 Enabling Authentication in `settings.py`

Modify `settings.py`:

python

```
REST_FRAMEWORK = {
    'DEFAULT_AUTHENTICATION_CLASSES': [

'rest_framework.authentication.SessionAuthentic
ation',

'rest_framework.authentication.TokenAuthenticat
ion',
    ],
    'DEFAULT_PERMISSION_CLASSES': [

'rest_framework.permissions.IsAuthenticated',
    ],
}
```

This requires users to authenticate before accessing APIs.

15.3.2 Using API Tokens for Authentication

Run:

```sh

pip install djangorestframework authtoken
```

Add it to INSTALLED_APPS:

```python

INSTALLED_APPS += ['rest_framework.authtoken']
```

Run migrations:

```sh

python manage.py migrate
```

Now, each user will have an authentication token.

15.3.3 Creating and Using Tokens

Modify myapp/views.py:

python

```python
from rest_framework.authtoken.models import Token
from django.contrib.auth.models import User

# Generate a token for a user
user = User.objects.get(username="admin")
token, created = Token.objects.get_or_create(user=user)
print(token.key)
```

Clients must now include the token in API requests:

sh

```sh
curl -H "Authorization: Token your_token_here" http://127.0.0.1:8000/api/books/
```

Conclusion

In this chapter, you learned:

How Django REST Framework simplifies API development

How to use serializers and views to create APIs
How to secure APIs using authentication and permissions

Next, we'll explore **Django middleware and security best practices!**

CHAPTER 16

DJANGO MIDDLEWARE AND SECURITY BEST PRACTICES

Security is a critical aspect of web development. Django provides a robust framework for building secure web applications by including **middleware** for request/response handling and built-in protections against common web vulnerabilities like **CSRF** and **Clickjacking**.

In this chapter, you'll learn:
How Django middleware works
How to protect against Cross-Site Request Forgery (CSRF) and Clickjacking
Security settings and performance optimizations

16.1 Understanding Django Middleware

16.1.1 What is Middleware?

Middleware is a layer that sits between the request and response cycle. It is executed for each request that comes to

168

the Django app and can process both the request before it reaches the view and the response before it is returned to the user.

Common Middleware Uses:

- **Request handling**: Modify or log requests before they reach the view.
- **Response handling**: Modify the response before it's sent to the user.
- **Session handling**: Maintain user sessions.
- **Security**: Implement security features like CSRF protection, session expiry, etc.

16.1.2 Configuring Middleware in `settings.py`

Django includes several default middleware classes that handle common tasks. These middleware are listed in the MIDDLEWARE setting in `settings.py`:

python

```
MIDDLEWARE = [

'django.middleware.security.SecurityMiddleware'
,
```

```
'django.contrib.sessions.middleware.SessionMidd
leware',

'django.middleware.common.CommonMiddleware',

'django.middleware.csrf.CsrfViewMiddleware',

'django.contrib.auth.middleware.AuthenticationM
iddleware',

'django.contrib.messages.middleware.MessageMidd
leware',

'django.middleware.clickjacking.XFrameOptionsMi
ddleware',
]
```

Custom Middleware

You can create your own custom middleware by creating a Python class with the __init__ and __call__ methods:

python

```
class CustomMiddleware:
    def __init__(self, get_response):
        self.get_response = get_response

    def __call__(self, request):
```

```
print("Request received")
response = self.get_response(request)
print("Response generated")
return response
```

You can then add this to the MIDDLEWARE list.

16.2 Cross-Site Request Forgery (CSRF) and Clickjacking
Protection

16.2.1 What is CSRF?

CSRF attacks occur when a malicious user tricks an authenticated user into submitting a request that performs unwanted actions on a web application (e.g., transferring funds, changing settings).

Django's CSRF Protection

By default, Django provides **CSRF protection** for all POST, PUT, and DELETE requests. To activate CSRF protection, you must include {% csrf_token %} in your HTML form and include the **token** in the request.

How CSRF Protection Works

1. **Token Generation**: Each user session gets a unique CSRF token.
2. **Token Validation**: The token must be included in forms and matched when the form is submitted.

Example of a form with CSRF protection:

html

```html
<form method="POST">
    {% csrf_token %}
    <input type="text" name="username" required>
    <button type="submit">Submit</button>
</form>
```

Disabling CSRF Protection

If you need to disable CSRF protection for a specific view (not recommended), you can use the `@csrf_exempt` decorator:

python

```python
from     django.views.decorators.csrf     import
csrf_exempt

@csrf_exempt
def my_view(request):
    return HttpResponse("CSRF disabled for this
view.")
```

16.2.2 What is Clickjacking?

Clickjacking is a technique where an attacker can trick a user into clicking on something different from what they perceive, typically by using invisible or disguised frames.

Django's Clickjacking Protection

Django provides protection by preventing your site from being embedded in an iframe. This is done using the **X-Frame-Options** header, which is automatically included in your response headers by the `XFrameOptionsMiddleware`.

How to Configure Clickjacking Protection

Django uses the `X-Frame-Options` header to specify whether your site can be embedded in an iframe:

- **DENY**: Prevents the site from being embedded in any iframe.
- **SAMEORIGIN**: Allows the site to be embedded only in an iframe on the same domain.

In `settings.py`, you can set this middleware to **DENY** by default:

```python
```

```python
X_FRAME_OPTIONS = 'DENY'
```

16.3 Security Settings and Performance Optimizations

16.3.1 Securing Cookies and Sessions

Django offers several settings to secure **cookies** and **sessions,** which store sensitive user data.

- **Session Expiry**: Configure session timeout to ensure sessions are automatically closed after a period of inactivity:

```python
```

```python
SESSION_COOKIE_AGE = 3600    # Time in
seconds (1 hour)
```

- **Secure Cookies**: Enable secure cookies by setting them to be sent only over HTTPS:

```python
```

```python
SESSION_COOKIE_SECURE = True
CSRF_COOKIE_SECURE = True
```

- **HttpOnly Cookies**: Prevent JavaScript from accessing cookies, adding a layer of security against XSS attacks:

```python
python
```

```python
SESSION_COOKIE_HTTPONLY = True
CSRF_COOKIE_HTTPONLY = True
```

16.3.2 Secure Password Storage

Django uses **PBKDF2** by default to hash passwords. You can configure additional password hashing algorithms in settings.py to further improve security.

For example, to use **bcrypt**:

1. Install bcrypt:

```sh
sh
```

```sh
pip install bcrypt
```

2. Add it to settings.py:

```python
python
```

```
PASSWORD_HASHERS = [

'django.contrib.auth.hashers.BCryptSHA256
PasswordHasher',
]
```

16.3.3 Enabling SSL/TLS (HTTPS)

To ensure all communication between the client and server is encrypted, you should enable **SSL/TLS**.

1. **Redirect all traffic to HTTPS** by adding this to settings.py:

   python

   ```
   SECURE_SSL_REDIRECT = True
   ```

2. **Use HSTS** (HTTP Strict Transport Security) to enforce HTTPS:

   python

   ```
   SECURE_HSTS_SECONDS = 31536000  # 1 year
   SECURE_HSTS_INCLUDE_SUBDOMAINS = True
   ```

3. **Set a secure cookie flag** for all cookies:

```
python
```

```
SECURE_BROWSER_XSS_FILTER = True
```

16.3.4 Performance Optimizations

To improve the performance of your Django application, consider the following optimizations:

- **Database Query Optimization**: Use `select_related` and `prefetch_related` to reduce the number of database queries.

  ```python
  queryset = Book.objects.select_related('author').all()
  ```

- **Caching**: Use Django's built-in caching mechanisms (e.g., `Memcached`, `Redis`) to cache frequently requested data.

  ```python
  CACHE_MIDDLEWARE_ALIAS = 'default'
  ```

```
CACHE_MIDDLEWARE_SECONDS = 600  # Cache for
10 minutes
```

- **Use Gzip Compression**: Enable Gzip to reduce the size of responses.

```python
MIDDLEWARE = [

'django.middleware.gzip.GZipMiddleware',
    # Other middleware
]
```

Conclusion

In this chapter, you learned: **How Django middleware works How to protect against CSRF and Clickjacking How to implement security best practices and performance optimizations**

Next, we'll explore **Django's template system and advanced features!**

CHAPTER 17

DEPLOYING DJANGO APPLICATIONS

Deploying your Django application to a live server is a crucial step in making your web application accessible to users. In this chapter, we will discuss how to deploy Django apps to popular hosting platforms such as **DigitalOcean**, **AWS**, and **Heroku**. We will also look at how to set up a **production environment**, configure **Docker** for containerization, and set up **CI/CD pipelines** for continuous deployment.

17.1 Hosting Django Apps on DigitalOcean, AWS, and Heroku

17.1.1 Hosting on DigitalOcean

DigitalOcean provides an easy and affordable way to deploy web applications. To host your Django app on **DigitalOcean**, follow these steps:

Step 1: Create a Droplet (Virtual Machine)

1. Go to **DigitalOcean** and create an account.
2. Click on **Create** and select **Droplet**.
3. Choose the **Ubuntu** image (or another OS if you prefer).
4. Choose the **plan** (for a small Django app, the basic $5/month plan should work).
5. Select your **data center region**.
6. Add your **SSH keys** for secure login.
7. Click **Create Droplet**.

Step 2: SSH into the Droplet

Once your droplet is created, you can SSH into it using the terminal:

sh

```
ssh root@your_droplet_ip
```

Step 3: Install Dependencies

Once logged in, you need to install the following dependencies:

sh

```
sudo apt update
```

```
sudo apt install python3-pip python3-dev libpq-
dev postgresql postgresql-contrib nginx curl
```

Step 4: Set Up the Django App

1. Clone your project from GitHub or upload it via SFTP.
2. Set up a **virtual environment** and install dependencies:

    sh

    ```
    python3 -m venv myenv
    source myenv/bin/activate
    pip install -r requirements.txt
    ```

Step 5: Configure Gunicorn and Nginx

Gunicorn is a production-ready WSGI server for serving your Django app, while Nginx will act as a reverse proxy.

1. Install Gunicorn:

    sh

    ```
    pip install gunicorn
    ```

2. Start Gunicorn:

    sh

    ```
    gunicorn            --workers           3
    yourproject.wsgi:application
    ```

3. Install Nginx and configure it to serve your Django app:

sh

```
sudo apt install nginx
sudo        nano        /etc/nginx/sites-
available/yourproject
```

Add the following configuration to the Nginx file:

nginx

```
server {
    listen 80;
    server_name your_droplet_ip;

    location / {
        proxy_pass http://127.0.0.1:8000;
        proxy_set_header Host $host;
        proxy_set_header        X-Real-IP
$remote_addr;
    }
}
```

Then enable the configuration:

sh

```
sudo        ln        -s        /etc/nginx/sites-
available/yourproject        /etc/nginx/sites-
enabled
sudo systemctl restart nginx
```

Your Django app is now hosted on DigitalOcean!

17.1.2 Hosting on AWS

AWS (Amazon Web Services) provides flexible and scalable infrastructure for deploying Django apps.

Step 1: Launch an EC2 Instance

1. Go to <u>AWS EC2</u> and create an account.
2. Launch an **EC2 instance** with an Ubuntu image.
3. Choose **t2.micro** for the free tier.
4. Configure security settings to allow HTTP (port 80) and SSH (port 22).

Step 2: SSH into the EC2 Instance

Once the instance is running, SSH into it:

```sh
ssh -i "your-key.pem" ubuntu@your-ec2-ip
```

Step 3: Install Dependencies

Install Python, PostgreSQL, Nginx, and Gunicorn as described in the **DigitalOcean** section above.

Step 4: Set Up Your Django App

Clone your Django app from a repository, set up a **virtual environment**, and install dependencies:

```sh
git clone your_repo_url
cd yourproject
python3 -m venv myenv
source myenv/bin/activate
pip install -r requirements.txt
```

Step 5: Configure Gunicorn and Nginx

Follow the same steps as for DigitalOcean to set up **Gunicorn** and **Nginx**.

17.1.3 Hosting on Heroku

Heroku is one of the easiest platforms for deploying Django apps without managing infrastructure.

Step 1: Install Heroku CLI

First, install the **Heroku CLI**:

```sh
```

```sh
curl https://cli-assets.heroku.com/install.sh |
sh
```

Step 2: Prepare Your App for Deployment

Make sure your Django app has:

- **requirements.txt** file.
- **Procfile** for Heroku to know how to run your app:

  ```makefile
  ```

  ```
  web: gunicorn yourproject.wsgi
  ```

Step 3: Push Your Code to Heroku

1. Login to Heroku:

   ```sh
   ```

   ```
   heroku login
   ```

2. Initialize a Git repository (if not already initialized):

   ```sh
   ```

185

```
git init
git add .
git commit -m "Initial commit"
```

3. Create a new app on Heroku:

```sh
heroku create your-app-name
```

4. Deploy to Heroku:

```sh
git push heroku master
```

5. Access your app:

```sh
heroku open
```

Your Django app is now deployed on Heroku!

17.2 Setting Up Production Environments

In production, there are a few additional configurations needed to make your Django app more secure and efficient.

17.2.1 Set DEBUG to False

In `settings.py`, ensure `DEBUG = False` for production:

```python

DEBUG = False
```

17.2.2 Configure Allowed Hosts

Set `ALLOWED_HOSTS` to include your domain or IP address:

```python

ALLOWED_HOSTS = ['yourdomain.com', 'your_ip',
'localhost']
```

17.2.3 Set Up a Database for Production

For production, you should use a more robust database, such as **PostgreSQL** or **MySQL**.

Install PostgreSQL:

187

sh

```
sudo apt install postgresql postgresql-contrib
```

Install psycopg2:

sh

```
pip install psycopg2
```

Modify settings.py to connect to the PostgreSQL database:

python

```
DATABASES = {
    'default': {
        'ENGINE':
'django.db.backends.postgresql',
        'NAME': 'yourdbname',
        'USER': 'yourusername',
        'PASSWORD': 'yourpassword',
        'HOST': 'localhost',
        'PORT': '5432',
    }
}
```

17.2.4 Set Up Static and Media Files

In production, **static** files (CSS, JS) and **media** files (uploads) must be served separately.

Use Nginx to serve them and configure **STATIC_ROOT** and **MEDIA_ROOT**:

python

```
STATIC_ROOT = "/path/to/static"
MEDIA_ROOT = "/path/to/media"
```

Run collectstatic to gather static files:

sh

```
python manage.py collectstatic
```

17.3 Using Docker and CI/CD for Django Projects

17.3.1 Using Docker for Containerization

Docker allows you to containerize your Django app, making it easy to deploy across different environments.

Step 1: Create a Dockerfile

Create a Dockerfile:

```
dockerfile

# Use official Python image
FROM python:3.9

# Set the working directory
WORKDIR /app

#  the dependencies
 requirements.txt /app/
RUN pip install -r requirements.txt

#  the application code
 . /app/

# Expose the port
EXPOSE 8000

# Run the application using Gunicorn
CMD ["gunicorn", "-w", "4", "-b", "0.0.0.0:8000",
"yourproject.wsgi:application"]
```

Step 2: Build and Run Docker Container

Build the image:

```sh
sh
```

```
docker build -t django-app .
```

Run the container:

```sh
```

```
docker run -p 8000:8000 django-app
```

Step 3: Push Docker Image to Docker Hub

Push your image to Docker Hub:

```sh
```

```
docker          tag          django-app
yourdockerhubusername/django-app
docker push yourdockerhubusername/django-app
```

17.3.2 Setting Up CI/CD Pipelines

Continuous Integration (CI) and Continuous Deployment (CD) automate the process of testing and deploying your app.

- Use **GitHub Actions**, **GitLab CI**, or **CircleCI** to create pipelines that automatically run tests, build Docker images, and deploy your app.

Conclusion

In this chapter, you learned:

How to deploy Django apps on DigitalOcean, AWS, and Heroku

How to set up a production environment for Django

How to use Docker and CI/CD for automating deployments

Next, we'll explore **Django's testing framework for writing unit tests and ensuring code quality!**

CHAPTER 18

COMPARING DJANGO AND FLASK – WHEN TO USE WHAT?

Both **Django** and **Flask** are powerful web frameworks for building Python-based web applications, but they have distinct strengths, use cases, and architectural philosophies. In this chapter, we'll compare the two frameworks, evaluate their strengths and weaknesses, and discuss how to choose the right one for your project. Additionally, we'll look at some real-world applications built with Django and Flask to understand where each framework excels.

18.1 Strengths and Weaknesses of Django and Flask

Django: The Full-Stack Framework

Strengths of Django:

- **Batteries-included approach**: Django comes with a lot of built-in features such as authentication, admin panel, ORM (Object-Relational Mapping), and form handling, which allows developers to build large-scale applications quickly.

- **Security**: Django is designed with security in mind. It has built-in protections against common vulnerabilities such as **CSRF**, **SQL injection**, and **Clickjacking**.
- **Scalability**: Django's architecture is built to scale, with features like query optimization, caching, and the ability to work with large databases efficiently.
- **Community and Documentation**: Django has a large and mature community with extensive documentation, tutorials, and third-party packages that help developers solve a wide range of problems.
- **Admin Interface**: The automatic admin interface is a huge productivity boost for building applications that require managing and interacting with large amounts of data.

Weaknesses of Django:

- **Monolithic structure**: Django follows a specific way of doing things. While it's flexible, developers can sometimes feel restricted in how they want to structure their project.
- **Learning curve**: Due to the amount of built-in functionality and configurations, Django can be overwhelming for beginners, especially when compared to the lightweight nature of Flask.

194

- **Less flexibility**: Django's opinionated approach can be limiting for smaller projects where flexibility is needed.

Flask: The Micro-Framework

Strengths of Flask:

- **Minimalistic and flexible**: Flask is a micro-framework, which means it provides the bare minimum tools to get your app running. It's highly flexible, allowing developers to pick their tools, libraries, and structure.
- **Simplicity and learning curve**: Flask is straightforward and easy to learn. It's ideal for smaller projects or beginners who want to get a web app up and running with minimal overhead.
- **Extensibility**: Flask allows developers to extend functionality with third-party libraries. You can add features like authentication, databases, or background tasks as needed.
- **Microservices and APIs**: Flask is often the framework of choice for creating **RESTful APIs** and **microservices** because of its lightweight nature and ease of integration with other systems.

Weaknesses of Flask:

- **Lack of built-in features**: Unlike Django, Flask doesn't come with as many built-in tools, so developers need to install external libraries and manually configure things like authentication, form handling, and database management.
- **Not suitable for large projects**: While Flask is great for small to medium projects, it can become harder to scale for large applications without significant custom configuration.
- **Security**: While Flask offers some security features, developers need to be more proactive in implementing security mechanisms compared to Django's more comprehensive security features.

18.2 Choosing the Right Framework for Your Project

When to Choose Django

Django is ideal for **larger projects**, **enterprise applications**, and **data-driven applications** that require a lot of built-in features. Some use cases where Django excels include:

- **Content Management Systems (CMS)** like WordPress clones (e.g., Wagtail)

- **E-commerce platforms** like Shopify alternatives
- **Social media platforms** or **community-driven apps** (e.g., Instagram, Pinterest)
- **Corporate websites** with admin interfaces, user management, and data-driven dashboards
- **Large-scale applications** with complex database models and relationships

Why Choose Django:

- If you need to get up and running quickly with a lot of built-in tools (authentication, admin, form handling).
- If you expect your application to grow in scale and complexity, and you need a framework that supports scalability out-of-the-box.
- If security and best practices are a priority and you want a framework that handles these for you.
- If you prefer a more structured, opinionated approach where you follow best practices out of the box.

When to Choose Flask

Flask is perfect for **small projects, API development**, and **microservices**. It's also a great choice if you need full flexibility in terms of architecture and design. Some use cases where Flask shines include:

- **Simple websites or personal projects** where you want complete control over the app's architecture
- **RESTful APIs** for mobile applications or third-party integrations
- **Prototyping and MVPs** where speed of development and flexibility are key
- **Microservices** where each service is lightweight and independently deployable
- **Small-scale applications** with simple business logic

Why Choose Flask:

- If you want a lightweight framework with minimal overhead and the freedom to choose your tools.
- If you're working on small projects or applications that don't require a lot of built-in features.
- If you need to build an API or microservice and want something minimalistic that doesn't impose any structure on your codebase.
- If you want flexibility and prefer to make decisions on how you organize and structure your code.

18.3 Case Studies of Real-World Applications Using Django and Flask

Case Study 1: Instagram (Django)

Instagram, one of the most popular social media platforms, is built using **Django**. Instagram needed a framework that could scale to handle millions of users and support complex relationships (e.g., posts, comments, likes, followers) between them. Django's ORM, admin interface, and built-in authentication allowed Instagram's developers to focus on the core business logic while Django took care of many essential backend functionalities.

Why Django:

- Instagram required a robust and secure system with features like authentication, scalability, and a powerful ORM for handling complex data relationships.
- Django's batteries-included philosophy allowed Instagram to develop quickly without reinventing the wheel.

Case Study 2: Pinterest (Django)

Pinterest, the visual discovery engine, is another example of a large-scale platform built using **Django**. The app deals with millions of users and images, requiring Django's efficient handling of database queries, templating, and authentication.

Why Django:

- Pinterest needed a stable and scalable framework that could manage a large amount of user-generated content and media.
- Django's built-in features such as the ORM, security mechanisms, and scalability made it the ideal choice for a growing platform like Pinterest.

Case Study 3: Uber (Flask)

Uber, the ride-sharing service, uses **Flask** for building many of its backend microservices. Flask's lightweight nature and ability to scale with small, independent services made it an excellent choice for Uber's complex and distributed system.

Why Flask:

- Uber's microservices architecture required a framework that was simple, flexible, and fast.
- Flask's extensibility allowed Uber to add the necessary functionality for their various microservices, while keeping each service lightweight.

Case Study 4: Stripe (Flask)

Stripe, a popular online payment processing company, uses **Flask** for some of its internal APIs and services. Stripe needed a simple, minimalistic framework that could be used to quickly build APIs for its payment system.

Why Flask:

- Stripe needed to build fast, flexible APIs with minimal overhead.
- Flask's lightweight and flexible nature made it the ideal choice for building small, independent APIs.

Conclusion

In this chapter, you learned:
The strengths and weaknesses of Django and Flask

How to choose the right framework for your project Real-world case studies of applications built with Django and Flask

Django is ideal for large, data-driven, and secure applications, while Flask shines for smaller, flexible, and API-centric projects. The choice between Django and Flask ultimately depends on the size, complexity, and specific requirements of your project.

Next, we'll dive into **advanced Django features and optimization techniques** to help you build robust and efficient web applications!

CHAPTER 19

BUILDING A MULTI-USER BLOG (FLASK & DJANGO IMPLEMENTATION)

In this chapter, we will walk through building a simple **multi-user blog** using both **Flask** and **Django**. This will help us understand how the two frameworks handle similar tasks, and compare the **performance** and **ease of development**.

We'll start by implementing the blog with **Flask**, and then recreate the same blog with **Django**. Along the way, we will highlight the differences between the two frameworks in terms of setup, features, and code structure.

19.1 Creating a Blog with Flask

19.1.1 Project Setup

Start by setting up a new **Flask project**.

1. Create a new directory and set up a virtual environment:

   sh

   ```
   mkdir flask_blog
   cd flask_blog
   python3 -m venv venv
   source venv/bin/activate
   ```

2. Install **Flask** and **Flask-SQLAlchemy**:

   sh

   ```
   pip install flask flask_sqlalchemy
   ```

3. Create the basic project structure:

   pgsql

   ```
   flask_blog/
   ├── app.py
   ├── templates/
   │   └── index.html
   └── models.py
   ```

19.1.2 Define the Blog Model

In `models.py,` define the **User** and **Post** models:

python

```
from flask import Flask
from flask_sqlalchemy import SQLAlchemy

app = Flask(__name__)
app.config['SQLALCHEMY_DATABASE_URI']              =
'sqlite:///blog.db'
app.config['SQLALCHEMY_TRACK_MODIFICATIONS']    =
False
db = SQLAlchemy(app)

class User(db.Model):
    id = db.Column(db.Integer, primary_key=True)
    username       =       db.Column(db.String(100),
unique=True, nullable=False)
    email          =       db.Column(db.String(120),
unique=True, nullable=False)
    posts          =            db.relationship('Post',
backref='author', lazy=True)

class Post(db.Model):
    id = db.Column(db.Integer, primary_key=True)
    title       =          db.Column(db.String(100),
nullable=False)
    content = db.Column(db.Text, nullable=False)
```

```
    date_posted      =      db.Column(db.DateTime,
default=datetime.utcnow)
    user_id       =      db.Column(db.Integer,
db.ForeignKey('user.id'), nullable=False)

if __name__ == "__main__":
    db.create_all()
```

This defines two models: **User** and **Post**. Users can have multiple posts, and each post is associated with a user.

19.1.3 Implement Views and Routes

In `app.py`, create routes to handle blog posts and user interaction:

python

```
from flask import render_template, redirect,
url_for, request
from models import app, db, User, Post
from datetime import datetime

@app.route('/')
def home():
    posts = Post.query.all()
```

```
    return            render_template('index.html',
posts=posts)


@app.route('/create', methods=['GET', 'POST'])
def create_post():
    if request.method == 'POST':
        title = request.form['title']
        content = request.form['content']
        user_id = 1  # Assuming user_id 1 exists
(you can add more logic later)
        post           =           Post(title=title,
content=content, user_id=user_id)
        db.session.add(post)
        db.session.commit()
        return redirect(url_for('home'))
    return render_template('create_post.html')


if __name__ == "__main__":
    app.run(debug=True)
```

19.1.4 Create Templates

Create a simple **index.html** template in the templates/ folder to display posts:

html

```
<!DOCTYPE html>
```

```
<html>
<head>
    <title>Flask Blog</title>
</head>
<body>
    <h1>Blog Posts</h1>
    {% for post in posts %}
        <h2>{{ post.title }}</h2>
        <p>{{ post.content }}</p>
        <small>By User {{ post.user_id }} on {{
post.date_posted }}</small>
    {% endfor %}
    <a        href="{{      url_for('create_post')
}}">Create a New Post</a>
</body>
</html>
```

And a simple **create_post.html** template:

html

```
<!DOCTYPE html>
<html>
<head>
    <title>Create Post</title>
</head>
<body>
    <h1>Create a New Post</h1>
    <form method="POST">
        <label for="title">Title:</label>
```

```
        <input        type="text"        name="title"
required><br>
        <label for="content">Content:</label>
        <textarea                name="content"
required></textarea><br>
        <button type="submit">Post</button>
    </form>
</body>
</html>
```

19.1.5 Running the Application

Run the Flask app:

```sh
```

```
python app.py
```

Now, you can visit **http://127.0.0.1:5000/** to see your Flask blog in action.

19.2 Recreating the Blog with Django

19.2.1 Project Setup

Start by setting up a **Django project**.

1. Create a new directory and set up a virtual environment:

   sh

   ```
   mkdir django_blog
   cd django_blog
   python3 -m venv venv
   source venv/bin/activate
   ```

2. Install **Django** and **Django ORM**:

   sh

   ```
   pip install django
   ```

3. Create a new Django project:

   sh

   ```
   django-admin startproject blog_project
   cd blog_project
   ```

4. Create a new app for the blog:

   sh

   ```
   python manage.py startapp blog
   ```

19.2.2 Define the Blog Model

In `blog/models.py`, define the **User** and **Post** models:

python

```python
from django.db import models
from django.contrib.auth.models import User

class Post(models.Model):
    title = models.CharField(max_length=100)
    content = models.TextField()
    date_posted                              =
models.DateTimeField(auto_now_add=True)
    author       =          models.ForeignKey(User,
on_delete=models.CASCADE)

    def __str__(self):
        return self.title
```

19.2.3 Configure the Database

In `blog_project/settings.py`, set up the **SQLite database** and add `'blog'` to INSTALLED_APPS:

python

```python
INSTALLED_APPS = [
```

```
...
'blog',
]
```

Run migrations to create the database:

```sh
```

```
python manage.py migrate
```

19.2.4 Implement Views and URLs

In `blog/views.py`, implement the views for displaying and creating posts:

```python
```

```python
from django.shortcuts import render, redirect
from .models import Post
from django.contrib.auth.models import User
from django.http import HttpResponse

def home(request):
    posts = Post.objects.all()
    return      render(request,      'home.html',
{'posts': posts})

def create_post(request):
```

212

```
if request.method == 'POST':
    title = request.POST['title']
    content = request.POST['content']
    user = User.objects.get(id=1)
    post            =            Post(title=title,
content=content, author=user)
    post.save()
    return redirect('home')
return render(request, 'create_post.html')
```

In `blog_project/urls.py`, **define URLs for the views:**

python

```
from django.urls import path
from blog import views

urlpatterns = [
    path('', views.home, name='home'),
    path('create/',            views.create_post,
name='create_post'),
]
```

19.2.5 Create Templates

Create `home.html` and `create_post.html` templates inside the `blog/templates/` directory, similar to the Flask templates.

19.2.6 Running the Application

Run the Django app:

```sh
```

```
python manage.py runserver
```

Now, you can visit **http://127.0.0.1:8000/** to see your Django blog in action.

19.3 Comparing Performance and Ease of Development

Performance Comparison

- **Flask**: Flask is minimalistic and lightweight, which can give it a slight performance edge for smaller applications. Since Flask doesn't come with built-in features like an ORM, it can be more flexible and faster for small projects.
- **Django**: Django is optimized for larger-scale applications with more complex requirements. Its additional features (like the ORM, authentication, and admin panel) come with overhead, which can make it slightly slower than

Flask for very small apps but is optimized for large data sets and complex queries.

Ease of Development

- **Flask**: Flask is easier to get started with because of its simple structure and minimal setup. Developers have more freedom to structure the application the way they want, but that also means more work for tasks that Django would automate.
- **Django**: Django is better for larger projects that need many built-in features (like authentication, admin panels, or database management). However, it comes with a steeper learning curve because of its opinionated way of structuring applications.

Conclusion

In this chapter, you:

- Built a **multi-user blog** using both **Flask** and **Django**.
- Compared **Flask**'s flexibility and simplicity with **Django**'s feature-rich, structured approach.
- Evaluated the **performance** and **ease of development** for both frameworks.

Both frameworks have their strengths and are suited for different types of projects. Flask is ideal for small, quick projects or APIs, while Django is perfect for larger, more complex applications requiring more built-in features and a more structured approach.

CHAPTER 20

SCALING APPLICATIONS – PERFORMANCE AND CACHING

As applications grow, they need to be optimized for **performance** and **scalability**. Whether you're using **Flask** or **Django**, there are various strategies for improving speed, managing high traffic loads, and ensuring that your application runs smoothly even as user numbers grow.

In this chapter, we'll explore:
How to use caching with Flask and Django Techniques for load balancing and database optimization
Managing large-scale web applications

20.1 Using Caching with Flask and Django

20.1.1 Caching in Flask

Caching is a technique used to store frequently accessed data in memory to speed up repeated access. In Flask, we can use **Flask-Caching** to add caching support.

Step 1: Install Flask-Caching

Run:

sh

```
pip install flask-caching
```

Step 2: Configure Flask-Caching

In your `app.py` file, set up caching:

python

```
from flask import Flask
from flask_caching import Cache

app = Flask(__name__)
app.config['CACHE_TYPE'] = 'simple'  # Simple in-
memory cache
cache = Cache(app)

@app.route('/')
@cache.cached(timeout=60)  # Cache this route for
60 seconds
def home():
```

```
return "This is a cached response!"
```

With this configuration, the response for the / route will be cached for 60 seconds. Any subsequent requests within that time will get the cached data.

Cache Types in Flask

- **Simple Cache**: Stores data in memory.
- **Redis Cache**: Uses Redis for distributed caching.
- **Memcached**: An in-memory caching system that supports multi-server caching.

20.1.2 Caching in Django

Django also supports caching out of the box. It provides various caching strategies, from file-based caching to more advanced methods using **Redis** and **Memcached**.

Step 1: Install Cache Backends

Install **Redis** if using it as the cache backend:

```sh
sh
```

```
pip install django-redis
```

Step 2: Configure Caching in `settings.py`

To use **file-based caching**:

python

```python
CACHES = {
    'default': {
        'BACKEND':
'django.core.cache.backends.filebased.FileBased
Cache',
        'LOCATION': '/path/to/cache/directory',
    }
}
```

To use **Redis** for caching:

python

```python
CACHES = {
    'default': {
        'BACKEND':
'django_redis.cache.RedisCache',
        'LOCATION':  'redis://127.0.0.1:6379/1',
# Redis server URL
        'OPTIONS': {
            'CLIENT_CLASS':
'django_redis.client.DefaultClient'
        }
    }
```

}

Step 3: Caching Views

In Django, you can use **cache_page** to cache views:

python

```
from     django.views.decorators.cache     import
cache_page

@cache_page(60 * 15)   # Cache the page for 15
minutes
def home(request):
    return render(request, "home.html")
```

Advanced Caching in Django

- **Template Fragment Caching**: Cache parts of a template to avoid re-rendering static content.
- **Database Query Caching**: Cache query results for faster access to frequently accessed data.

20.2 Load Balancing and Database Optimization

20.2.1 Load Balancing

Load balancing is a strategy used to distribute incoming traffic across multiple servers to ensure that no single server is overwhelmed. This helps in **scaling horizontally**.

Step 1: Set Up Multiple Application Servers

1. **Horizontal Scaling**: Deploy multiple instances of your application on different servers or containers (using Docker).
2. **Load Balancer**: Use a load balancer like **Nginx** or **HAProxy** to distribute requests evenly across the servers.

Step 2: Nginx as a Load Balancer

In Nginx, you can configure the load balancer to direct traffic to multiple backend servers:

```nginx
http {
    upstream app_servers {
        server app_server1:8000;
        server app_server2:8000;
        server app_server3:8000;
    }

    server {
        location / {
```

```
        proxy_pass http://app_servers;
        proxy_set_header Host $host;
        proxy_set_header          X-Real-IP
$remote_addr;
        }
    }
}
```

Nginx will now distribute incoming traffic among the backend servers (app_server1, app_server2, app_server3).

20.2.2 Database Optimization

Step 1: Use Database Indexing

Create **indexes** on frequently queried fields to speed up database access. In **Django**, you can add an index to a model field like this:

python

```python
class Post(models.Model):
    title    =    models.CharField(max_length=100,
db_index=True)
    content = models.TextField()
```

This will add an index on the `title` column to improve query performance when searching by title.

Step 2: Query Optimization

- **Use `select_related` and `prefetch_related` in Django**: These Django ORM functions optimize database queries when working with related models (e.g., ForeignKeys, ManyToMany).

```python
python

posts                                      =
Post.objects.select_related('author').all
()
```

- **Database Sharding**: Divide large databases into smaller, more manageable pieces, each hosted on different servers, to handle high loads.

Step 3: Database Replication

Use **database replication** to ensure high availability and load distribution. In **MySQL** or **PostgreSQL**, you can set up a master-slave replication system where writes go to the master and reads go to the slaves.

20.3 Managing Large-Scale Web Applications

Managing large-scale applications involves several strategies beyond caching and load balancing. Here are some additional best practices:

20.3.1 Microservices Architecture

Instead of having a monolithic architecture, break the application into smaller, independent **microservices**. Each service is responsible for a single feature or set of features, making the application easier to scale and manage.

For example, you could separate the blog functionality, user authentication, and file uploads into separate microservices.

20.3.2 Asynchronous Task Processing

For long-running tasks (e.g., sending emails, processing images), use **task queues** like **Celery** to handle these operations asynchronously, offloading them from the main request-response cycle.

In Django, you can use **Celery** with **RabbitMQ** or **Redis** as the message broker to run background tasks efficiently.

20.3.3 Caching with CDNs (Content Delivery Networks)

Use a **CDN** like **Cloudflare** or **Amazon CloudFront** to offload static content (e.g., images, CSS, JavaScript) and serve it from multiple geographic locations, improving page load speed and reducing server load.

Conclusion

In this chapter, you learned:
How to use caching with Flask and Django to optimize performance
Load balancing techniques to distribute traffic across multiple servers
Database optimization strategies like indexing, query optimization, and replication
Best practices for managing large-scale web applications, including microservices, task queues, and CDNs

By implementing these strategies, you can ensure that your web applications are fast, reliable, and scalable, even under high traffic loads.

CHAPTER 21

INTEGRATING FRONTEND FRAMEWORKS (REACT, VUE, AND DJANGO/FLASK)

As modern web development increasingly relies on **single-page applications (SPAs)**, integrating **frontend frameworks** like **React** and **Vue** with **backend frameworks** like **Django** and **Flask** is essential. These integrations allow you to create highly interactive, dynamic user interfaces while keeping the backend logic and database management streamlined.

In this chapter, we will cover:
How Django and Flask work with React and Vue
Setting up a frontend-backend connection
REST API vs. GraphQL with Django and Flask

21.1 How Django and Flask Work with React and Vue

Both **React** and **Vue** are powerful frontend frameworks that can be integrated with Django and Flask through **APIs**. Typically, the backend (Django/Flask) serves data via **REST APIs** or **GraphQL**, while the frontend (React/Vue) communicates with the backend asynchronously to update the UI.

21.1.1 Django with React

Django can be easily integrated with React by serving the React app as a **static file** and using **Django REST framework (DRF)** to handle the backend API requests.

Step 1: Set up Django with React

1. Create a **Django project** and a **React project**:

   sh

   ```
   django-admin startproject myproject
   cd myproject
   python manage.py startapp blog
   npx create-react-app frontend
   ```

2. Install **Django REST Framework** for serving the API:

```sh
```

```sh
pip install djangorestframework
```

3. In your Django project, configure **settings.py** to include rest_framework:

```python
```

```python
INSTALLED_APPS = [
    'rest_framework',
    'blog',
    'django.contrib.staticfiles',
]
```

4. Create a **basic API endpoint** in Django to serve data:

```python
```

```python
# blog/views.py
from rest_framework.views import APIView
from rest_framework.response import Response
from .models import Post
from .serializers import PostSerializer
```

229

```python
class PostList(APIView):
    def get(self, request):
        posts = Post.objects.all()
        serializer = PostSerializer(posts,
many=True)
        return Response(serializer.data)
```

And add a route to your **urls.py**:

```
python
```

```python
from django.urls import path
from .views import PostList

urlpatterns = [
    path('api/posts/',
PostList.as_view()),
]
```

5. Set up **React to communicate with Django**: In the React app (`frontend/src/App.js`), you can fetch data from Django using **Axios** or **fetch**:

```
javascript
```

```javascript
import React, { useEffect, useState } from 'react';

function App() {
```

```
const [posts, setPosts] = useState([]);

useEffect(() => {

fetch("http://127.0.0.1:8000/api/posts/")
    .then(response => response.json())
    .then(data => setPosts(data));
}, []);

return (
  <div>
    <h1>Blog Posts</h1>
    {posts.map(post => (
      <div key={post.id}>
        <h3>{post.title}</h3>
        <p>{post.content}</p>
      </div>
    ))}
  </div>
);
}

export default App;
```

6. **Run both the Django backend and React frontend**:

   o   Start the Django server:

   ```sh
   sh
   ```

```
python manage.py runserver
```

- o Start the React app:

```sh
```

```
npm start
```

Now your React app should be able to fetch data from Django and render it on the page.

21.1.2 Flask with React

Flask, like Django, can also serve as the backend for a React app, with the **Flask API** serving the data, and React managing the frontend.

Step 1: Set up Flask with React

1. Create a **Flask project** and a **React project**:

```sh
```

```
flask new myproject
cd myproject
npx create-react-app frontend
```

2. Install **Flask-CORS** for handling cross-origin requests between the frontend and backend:

```sh
```

```
pip install flask-cors
```

3. In your **Flask app**, define an API endpoint:

```python
```

```
from flask import Flask, jsonify
from flask_cors import CORS

app = Flask(__name__)
CORS(app)

posts = [
    {"id": 1, "title": "Post 1", "content":
"Content of post 1"},
    {"id": 2, "title": "Post 2", "content":
"Content of post 2"},
]

@app.route('/api/posts', methods=['GET'])
def get_posts():
    return jsonify(posts)

if __name__ == '__main__':
```

```
app.run(debug=True)
```

4. Set up **React to communicate with Flask** as shown in the Django example, using **fetch** or **Axios**.

Step 2: Run both Flask and React

- Start the Flask server:

```sh
flask run
```

- Start the React app:

```sh
npm start
```

21.1.3 Vue.js with Django/Flask

Vue.js, like React, is another powerful frontend framework that can easily be integrated with both Django and Flask.

- **Vue with Django**: Similar to React, Vue communicates with Django through a **REST API**. The steps are the same as the Django/React setup,

234

where Vue makes AJAX requests to Django's backend and renders the data.

- **Vue with Flask**: Just like React, Vue can fetch data from Flask via RESTful API calls. You can follow the same approach as the Flask/React example above, replacing React with Vue in the frontend.

21.2 Setting Up a Frontend-Backend Connection

To connect the **frontend** (React/Vue) with the **backend** (Django/Flask), you typically use **AJAX** (Asynchronous JavaScript and XML) requests to fetch data from the backend. This allows the frontend to remain interactive without reloading the page.

Frontend-Backend Communication with REST APIs

Step 1: Enable Cross-Origin Resource Sharing (CORS)

Both Django and Flask need to handle cross-origin requests when the frontend is running on a different domain or port from the backend.

- **In Django,** add **django-cors-headers** to INSTALLED_APPS and MIDDLEWARE in settings.py:

python

```python
INSTALLED_APPS = [
    'corsheaders',
    # Other apps
]

MIDDLEWARE = [

'corsheaders.middleware.CorsMiddleware',
    # Other middleware
]

CORS_ALLOWED_ORIGINS = [
    'http://localhost:3000',      # React
frontend
]
```

- **In Flask,** use **Flask-CORS**:

python

```python
from flask_cors import CORS
CORS(app)
```

21.3 REST API vs. GraphQL with Django and Flask

21.3.1 REST API

REST (Representational State Transfer) is an architectural style for building APIs. It uses standard HTTP methods (GET, POST, PUT, DELETE) to interact with resources.

- **Advantages of REST**:
    - Simple to implement and widely supported.
    - Can work with any frontend framework (React, Vue, Angular).
    - Ideal for applications where the data is consistent and the requests are simple.
- **Using REST with Django and Flask**: Both frameworks provide tools to quickly build and expose RESTful APIs, with Django using **Django REST Framework (DRF)** and Flask using **Flask-RESTful**.

Example RESTful API Request:

- **GET** request to fetch blog posts:

```javascript
javascript
```

```
fetch("http://127.0.0.1:8000/api/posts/")
  .then(response => response.json())
  .then(data => console.log(data));
```

21.3.2 GraphQL

GraphQL is an alternative to REST that allows clients to request only the data they need, and it provides more flexibility in how data is queried.

- **Advantages of GraphQL**:
  - o Efficient and flexible: Clients can query only the fields they need.
  - o Reduces over-fetching and under-fetching of data.
  - o Suitable for complex data models where relationships between entities are intricate.
- **Using GraphQL with Django**: To integrate **GraphQL** with Django, you can use libraries like **Graphene-Django**:

```sh
pip install graphene-django
```

- **Using GraphQL with Flask**: Flask can be integrated with GraphQL using **Graphene-Flask**:

sh

```
pip install graphene flask-graphql
```

Example GraphQL Query:

- **Query to fetch blog posts**:

graphql

```
query {
  posts {
    title
    content
  }
}
```

Conclusion

In this chapter, you learned: **How to integrate React and Vue with Django and Flask** for building modern, dynamic web applications. **How to set up frontend-backend connections** using **REST APIs** and **GraphQL**.

The differences between REST and GraphQL in terms of data fetching and query flexibility.

Both **React** and **Vue** are powerful tools that can be used with either **Django** or **Flask** to build rich, interactive web applications. The choice between **REST** and **GraphQL** depends on the specific needs of your project.

CHAPTER 22

WEBSOCKETS AND REAL-TIME APPLICATIONS

Real-time applications are becoming increasingly popular, especially with the rise of applications that require **instant communication**, such as **chat applications**, **live updates**, and **notifications**. WebSockets provide a full-duplex communication channel over a single, long-lived connection, which is ideal for these types of applications.

In this chapter, we will explore:
How to implement WebSockets in Django and Flask
Using Django Channels for real-time applications
Creating a simple chat application example

22.1 Implementing WebSockets in Django and Flask

22.1.1 WebSockets Overview

WebSocket is a protocol that enables **bidirectional communication** between a client (e.g., a web browser) and a server. Unlike traditional HTTP requests, which are stateless and open a new connection for each request, WebSockets allow you to open a persistent connection that can handle multiple interactions over time.

WebSocket Basics:

- **Persistent connection**: WebSocket establishes a connection that remains open.
- **Real-time updates**: Both the server and client can send data to each other at any time.
- **Efficient for real-time applications**: WebSockets are ideal for use cases like live chats, notifications, and real-time dashboards.

22.1.2 WebSockets in Django

Django doesn't support WebSockets natively, but you can use **Django Channels** to handle WebSockets.

Step 1: Install Django Channels

Install Django Channels using **pip**:

sh

```
pip install channels
```

Step 2: Configure Django Channels in `settings.py`

In your **Django project's `settings.py`**, add `'channels'` to `INSTALLED_APPS` and set **Channels** as the default ASGI application:

```python
python
```

```python
INSTALLED_APPS = [
    ...
    'channels',
    ...
]
```

```python
ASGI_APPLICATION                                =
'yourproject.asgi.application'
```

Step 3: Create an ASGI Application

In your project's root directory, create an `asgi.py` file:

```python
python
```

```python
import os
from           django.core.asgi           import
get_asgi_application
from channels.routing import ProtocolTypeRouter,
URLRouter
from channels.auth import AuthMiddlewareStack
```

```
os.environ.setdefault('DJANGO_SETTINGS_MODULE',
'yourproject.settings')

application = ProtocolTypeRouter({
    "http": get_asgi_application(),
    "websocket": AuthMiddlewareStack(
        URLRouter([
            # WebSocket routes
        ])
    ),
})
```

Step 4: Implement WebSocket Consumers

Create a **consumer** that will handle the WebSocket connections. A **consumer** is a Python class or function that handles WebSocket events.

In `chat/consumers.py`:

python

```
import json
from      channels.generic.websocket      import
AsyncWebsocketConsumer

class ChatConsumer(AsyncWebsocketConsumer):
    async def connect(self):
        self.room_name = "chat_room"
```

```
        self.room_group_name                    =
f'chat_{self.room_name}'

        # Join room group
        await self.channel_layer.group_add(
            self.room_group_name,
            self.channel_name
        )
        await self.accept()

    async def disconnect(self, close_code):
        # Leave room group
        await self.channel_layer.group_discard(
            self.room_group_name,
            self.channel_name
        )

    # Receive message from WebSocket
    async def receive(self, text_data):
        text_data_json = json.loads(text_data)
        message = text_data_json['message']

        # Send message to room group
        await self.channel_layer.group_send(
            self.room_group_name,
            {
                'type': 'chat_message',
                'message': message
            }
```

```
        )

    # Receive message from room group
    async def chat_message(self, event):
        message = event['message']

        # Send message to WebSocket
        await self.send(text_data=json.dumps({
            'message': message
        }))
```

Step 5: Set Up Channels Layer (Redis)

To handle real-time messaging, Channels needs a **channel layer**. Redis is commonly used for this purpose.

Install **Redis** and the Django Channels Redis package:

sh

```
pip install channels_redis
```

In **settings.py**, configure the **CHANNEL_LAYERS**:

python

```
CHANNEL_LAYERS = {
    'default': {
        'BACKEND':
'channels_redis.core.RedisChannelLayer',
```

```
'CONFIG': {
    "hosts": [('127.0.0.1', 6379)],
    },
},
}
```

Step 6: Running the Django Application with Channels

To run your Django application with **Channels**, use `daphne` or **ASGI** server (instead of `runserver`):

sh

```
pip install daphne
daphne yourproject.asgi:application
```

Now your Django app supports WebSockets.

22.1.3 WebSockets in Flask

Flask itself doesn't provide WebSocket support, but you can use **Flask-SocketIO** to integrate WebSockets into your Flask app.

Step 1: Install Flask-SocketIO

Install **Flask-SocketIO**:

sh

```
pip install flask-socketio
```

Step 2: Set Up Flask with SocketIO

In `app.py`, set up **SocketIO**:

python

```python
from flask import Flask, render_template
from flask_socketio import SocketIO, send

app = Flask(__name__)
socketio = SocketIO(app)

@app.route('/')
def index():
    return render_template('index.html')

@socketio.on('message')
def handle_message(msg):
    print('Received message: ' + msg)
    send(msg, broadcast=True)

if __name__ == '__main__':
    socketio.run(app, debug=True)
```

Step 3: Create a Frontend WebSocket Client

In `templates/index.html`:

html

```html
<!DOCTYPE html>
<html>
<head>
    <title>Flask WebSocket</title>
    <script
src="https://cdnjs.cloudflare.com/ajax/libs/soc
ket.io/4.0.0/socket.io.min.js"></script>
</head>
<body>
    <h1>Flask WebSocket</h1>
    <input type="text" id="message">
    <button
onclick="sendMessage()">Send</button>

    <ul id="messages"></ul>

    <script>
        var socket = io();

        // Receive message from Flask backend
        socket.on('message', function(msg) {
            var             li             =
document.createElement("li");
            li.textContent = msg;

document.getElementById("messages").appendChild
(li);
```

```
        });

        // Send message to backend
        function sendMessage() {
            var          message          =
document.getElementById("message").value;
            socket.send(message);
        }
    </script>
</body>
</html>
```

22.2 Using Django Channels for Real-Time Applications

22.2.1 Implementing a Chat Application with Django Channels

You can create a simple chat application using **Django Channels** and WebSockets. Here's a recap of the necessary steps for the chat app:

1. **Install and configure Channels**.
2. **Create a consumer to handle WebSocket connections** (like in the previous example).
3. **Set up a room group** to handle multiple users in the same chat room.

4. **Use the channel layer** (Redis) to manage communication between users.

Once all configurations are in place, you can handle real-time communication between users, and messages sent by one user will be broadcast to others in real time.

22.3 Chat Application Example

Here is a simplified structure of how a **chat application** might work using **WebSockets**.

Backend (Django with Channels)

- WebSocket connection is established using **Django Channels**.
- The `ChatConsumer` class listens for incoming messages and broadcasts them to other connected users.
- Redis is used as the **channel layer** to facilitate communication between users in real time.

Frontend (HTML/JavaScript)

- The frontend creates a WebSocket connection to the backend.

- It listens for messages from other users and displays them dynamically on the page.
- It allows the user to send messages to the backend, which then broadcasts them to other users.

Conclusion

In this chapter, you learned: **How to implement WebSockets** in both **Django** and **Flask** to handle real-time communication. **How to use Django Channels** for real-time applications like a chat application. **How to create a simple chat application** using WebSockets in Django and Flask.

WebSockets enable building highly interactive, real-time web applications, and with Django Channels and Flask-SocketIO, you can easily add WebSocket support to your projects.

CHAPTER 23

TESTING AND DEBUGGING DJANGO & FLASK APPS

Testing and debugging are critical components of the development process. Properly tested applications are more reliable, maintainable, and easier to scale. In this chapter, we'll cover: **Unit testing and integration testing Debugging common Flask and Django errors Using testing libraries like Pytest and Unittest**

By the end of this chapter, you'll be comfortable with writing tests and debugging errors in both **Django** and **Flask** apps.

23.1 Unit Testing and Integration Testing

23.1.1 Unit Testing

Unit tests focus on testing individual functions or components of your application in isolation. These tests are typically small, fast, and designed to test the **business logic** of your application.

Example of Unit Testing in Flask

In Flask, you can use **Python's built-in `unittest` module** to write tests for your app.

```python
python

import unittest
from app import app

class FlaskTestCase(unittest.TestCase):
    def setUp(self):
        self.app = app.test_client()
        self.app.testing = True

    def test_home_page(self):
        response = self.app.get('/')
        self.assertEqual(response.status_code, 200)
        self.assertIn(b'Welcome', response.data)

if __name__ == '__main__':
    unittest.main()
```

Steps:

1. **setUp()**: This method runs before every test case to set up the test environment. In this example, it sets up a test client for the Flask app.

2. **Test Method**: Each test method (like `test_home_page`) verifies a specific behavior. Here, it checks that the home page returns a **200 status code** and contains the word "Welcome".

3. **Running the Tests**: To run the tests, execute the file using `python -m unittest test_filename.py`.

Example of Unit Testing in Django

Django includes a built-in testing framework that uses `unittest` under the hood. Here's how you can write unit tests for Django:

```python
python

from django.test import TestCase
from django.urls import reverse

class TestHomePage(TestCase):
    def test_home_page_status(self):
        response                        =
self.client.get(reverse('home'))
```

255

```
        self.assertEqual(response.status_code,
200)
        self.assertContains(response, 'Welcome')
```

- **TestCase**: A subclass of `unittest.TestCase` designed specifically for testing Django apps.
- **self.client.get()**: Makes an HTTP GET request to the provided URL.
- **Assertions**: `assertEqual()` checks that the response status is 200, and `assertContains()` ensures the response contains the text "Welcome".

23.1.2 Integration Testing

Integration tests are broader and test how multiple components of your application work together. They check interactions between the backend, database, and frontend. In web applications, integration tests often involve sending HTTP requests and checking the resulting responses.

Integration Testing in Flask

In Flask, integration testing is usually done by sending HTTP requests using the test client:

```python
```

```
from app import app
import unittest

class FlaskTestCase(unittest.TestCase):
    def test_integration(self):
        response                          =
app.test_client().post('/create',
data=dict(title="Test", content="Test Content"))
        self.assertEqual(response.status_code,
200)
        self.assertIn(b'Post              created
successfully', response.data)

if __name__ == '__main__':
    unittest.main()
```

Integration Testing in Django

In Django, integration tests can be written by interacting with views and checking database entries:

```python
from django.test import TestCase
from django.urls import reverse
from .models import Post

class PostCreateTestCase(TestCase):
    def test_post_creation(self):
```

```
        response                        =
self.client.post(reverse('create_post'),
{'title': 'Test', 'content': 'Test Content'})
        self.assertEqual(response.status_code,
302)   # Redirect after POST

self.assertTrue(Post.objects.filter(title='Test
').exists())
```

- **reverse()**: This function generates URLs based on view names.
- **assertTrue()**: Checks that a `Post` object exists in the database with the title "Test".

23.2 Debugging Common Flask and Django Errors

23.2.1 Debugging Flask Errors

Flask provides a built-in debugger that displays helpful error messages and stack traces when something goes wrong.

Common Flask Errors

1. **404 Not Found**: This error usually happens when the URL route does not exist or is misspelled.
   o **Fix**: Double-check the route decorators and ensure the URL is correctly defined in the app.

2. **500 Internal Server Error**: This indicates an issue with the server or the application itself, often due to errors in the code.

   o **Fix**: Use Flask's **debug mode** (`app.debug = True`) to get more detailed error messages.

3. **Template Rendering Errors**: If you encounter issues rendering templates, Flask will usually output a helpful error message with the exact location of the issue.

   o **Fix**: Check the template for missing or incorrectly named variables.

23.2.2 Debugging Django Errors

Django also has a built-in **debug mode** that provides detailed error messages in the browser when something goes wrong.

Common Django Errors

1. **404 Not Found**: This error happens if the URL path is not registered properly.

   o **Fix**: Ensure the URL patterns in `urls.py` are correct and that the view exists.

2. **500 Internal Server Error**: A generic error indicating that something went wrong on the server.

o **Fix**: Check the server logs and Django's `debug` messages for more details. Run the application with `python manage.py runserver` and inspect the stack trace for further insight.

3. **Database Errors**: Errors related to model relationships, missing fields, or migrations can show up during development.

o **Fix**: Run `python manage.py makemigrations` and `python manage.py migrate` to ensure that your database is properly synced with the models.

23.3 Using Testing Libraries like Pytest and Unittest

23.3.1 Pytest

Pytest is a powerful testing framework that extends `unittest` and provides additional features, such as easy setup and teardown, fixtures, and advanced assertions.

Setting Up Pytest in Flask

1. Install **pytest**:

sh

```
pip install pytest
```

2. Create a test file, for example, `test_app.py`:

```python
python

import pytest
from app import app

@pytest.fixture
def client():
    with app.test_client() as client:
        yield client

def test_home(client):
    response = client.get('/')
    assert response.status_code == 200
    assert b'Welcome' in response.data
```

3. Run the tests with:

```sh
sh

pytest
```

Setting Up Pytest in Django

1. Install **pytest-django**:

```sh
sh
```

261

```
pip install pytest-django
```

2. Create a test file:

```python
import pytest
from django.urls import reverse

@pytest.mark.django_db
def test_home_page(client):
    response = client.get(reverse('home'))
    assert response.status_code == 200
    assert b'Welcome' in response.content
```

3. Run the tests with:

```sh
pytest
```

23.3.2 Unittest

Unittest is the built-in Python testing framework, which is simple and integrated into Python's standard library.

Example test with **Flask** using **Unittest**:

```python
import unittest
from app import app

class FlaskTestCase(unittest.TestCase):
    def setUp(self):
        self.app = app.test_client()

    def test_status_code(self):
        response = self.app.get('/')
        self.assertEqual(response.status_code,
200)

if __name__ == '__main__':
    unittest.main()
```

Using Unittest with Django

Example test with **Django** using **Unittest**:

```python
from django.test import TestCase
from django.urls import reverse
```

```
class TestHomePage(TestCase):
    def test_home_page(self):
        response                          =
self.client.get(reverse('home'))
        self.assertEqual(response.status_code,
200)


if __name__ == '__main__':
    unittest.main()
```

Conclusion

In this chapter, you learned: **How to write unit tests and integration tests** for Flask and Django applications.

How to debug common errors in both Flask and Django applications.

How to use testing libraries like Pytest and Unittest to write tests and run them efficiently.

By writing tests and using debugging tools, you ensure that your applications are robust, reliable, and easy to maintain.

CHAPTER 24

MACHINE LEARNING AND AI WITH DJANGO & FLASK

Machine learning (ML) and artificial intelligence (AI) are transforming the tech landscape, and integrating these powerful technologies into web applications is becoming more common. Django and Flask are both popular choices for deploying machine learning models and building AI-powered applications due to their flexibility and ease of use.

In this chapter, we'll cover:
How to use Flask and Django with TensorFlow and PyTorch
Building AI-powered applications
Deploying ML models with Django and Flask APIs

By the end of this chapter, you'll be able to integrate machine learning models into Django and Flask applications and deploy them for real-world use.

265

24.1 Using Flask and Django with TensorFlow & PyTorch

TensorFlow and PyTorch are the two most popular frameworks for developing machine learning models. Both can be used alongside Flask and Django to power AI-driven web applications.

24.1.1 Using TensorFlow with Flask

TensorFlow is an open-source framework for building machine learning models, particularly deep learning models. Flask can be used to serve TensorFlow models via REST APIs, allowing users to interact with the model.

Step 1: Install TensorFlow

First, you'll need to install **TensorFlow** and **Flask**:

sh

```
pip install tensorflow flask
```

Step 2: Create a Flask App to Serve the Model

Let's create a simple Flask application that serves a pre-trained model.

```
python
```

```python
from flask import Flask, jsonify, request
import tensorflow as tf
import numpy as np

app = Flask(__name__)

# Load the pre-trained model
model =
tf.keras.applications.MobileNetV2(weights='imag
enet')

@app.route('/predict', methods=['POST'])
def predict():
    image = request.files['image'].read()
    # Preprocess image (this part depends on the
model you're using)
    image = tf.image.decode_jpeg(image,
channels=3)
    image = tf.image.resize(image, [224, 224])  #
Resize to match input size
    image = tf.expand_dims(image, 0)  # Add batch
dimension

    # Make prediction
    predictions = model.predict(image)
    decoded_predictions =
tf.keras.applications.mobilenet_v2.decode_predi
ctions(predictions, top=1)[0][0]
```

267

```
    return              jsonify({'prediction':
decoded_predictions[1],              'confidence':
float(decoded_predictions[2])})


if __name__ == '__main__':
    app.run(debug=True)
```

Step 3: Testing the Model API

To test the API, send a POST request with an image to **/predict**. You can use **Postman** or **curl** to do this.

Example `curl` command:

```
sh
```

```
curl -X POST -F "image=@path_to_your_image.jpg"
http://127.0.0.1:5000/predict
```

This will return the model's predicted class label and confidence.

24.1.2 Using PyTorch with Django

PyTorch is another popular machine learning framework, particularly known for its flexibility and ease of use in research. Here's how to integrate a PyTorch model with Django.

Step 1: Install PyTorch and Django

sh

```
pip install torch torchvision django
```

Step 2: Set Up Django to Serve the Model

Create a **Django app** and configure a view that handles inference requests. Here's an example view that uses a pre-trained PyTorch model.

python

```
# views.py
from django.http import JsonResponse
import torch
from torchvision import models, transforms
from PIL import Image
import io

# Load the pre-trained model
model = models.resnet50(pretrained=True)
model.eval()

# Define image transformation
transform = transforms.Compose([
```

```
    transforms.Resize(256),
    transforms.CenterCrop(224),
    transforms.ToTensor(),
    transforms.Normalize(mean=[0.485,      0.456,
0.406], std=[0.229, 0.224, 0.225]),
])


def predict(request):
    if request.method == 'POST' and 'image' in
request.FILES:
        img = Image.open(request.FILES['image'])
        img = transform(img).unsqueeze(0)  # Add
batch dimension

        # Make prediction
        with torch.no_grad():
            outputs = model(img)
            _, predicted = torch.max(outputs, 1)

        return       JsonResponse({'prediction':
str(predicted.item())})

    return   JsonResponse({'error':   'No   image
uploaded'}, status=400)
```

Step 3: Testing the API

You can now test the Django API by sending a POST request
with an image to the `/predict` endpoint.

```bash
bash

curl -X POST -F "image=@path_to_your_image.jpg"
http://127.0.0.1:8000/predict
```

This will return the predicted class label for the uploaded image.

24.2 Building AI-Powered Applications

AI-powered applications can range from **image classification** to **natural language processing (NLP)** or **recommendation systems**. Here are some ideas for building AI applications with Flask and Django:

24.2.1 Image Classification

As demonstrated in the examples above, you can build an image classification app using pre-trained models like **MobileNetV2** (TensorFlow) or **ResNet50** (PyTorch). This application would allow users to upload an image, and the app will classify the image into one of many categories.

24.2.2 Sentiment Analysis

Sentiment analysis is a common NLP task where the goal is to determine whether a piece of text has a positive, negative, or neutral sentiment.

- **Flask and TensorFlow/PyTorch** can be used to serve a sentiment analysis model (e.g., BERT, GPT-3) to classify text based on sentiment.
- The frontend can take input from a user, send the request to the backend, and display the results in real time.

24.2.3 Recommendation Systems

A recommendation system suggests items to users based on their preferences. These systems are used in applications like **e-commerce** (Amazon), **video streaming** (Netflix), and **social media** (Facebook).

- You can build a recommendation engine using collaborative filtering or content-based filtering and deploy it using **Django/Flask**.
- Data is typically fetched from a database, processed using machine learning models, and served via APIs to recommend items in real time.

24.3 Deploying ML Models with Django and Flask APIs

24.3.1 Serving Models in Production

Once you have a trained machine learning model, the next step is to deploy it to production. Both **Django** and **Flask** can serve machine learning models via APIs, but here are some additional considerations:

Step 1: Model Serialization

When serving machine learning models, you'll want to serialize them for easy loading. Use `joblib` or `pickle` to save and load models.

Example:

```python
import joblib

# Save model
joblib.dump(model, 'model.pkl')

# Load model in the app
model = joblib.load('model.pkl')
```

Step 2: Containerizing the Application with Docker

Use **Docker** to containerize your application, making it easy to deploy on any server or cloud platform.

Create a **Dockerfile** for your Django or Flask app:

```
dockerfile

# Start from a Python base image
FROM python:3.8-slim

# Set the working directory
WORKDIR /app

# Install dependencies
 requirements.txt .
RUN pip install -r requirements.txt

#  the rest of the application
 . .


# Expose the port and start the app
EXPOSE 5000
CMD ["python", "app.py"]
```

Step 3: Deploying to Cloud

Deploy the application to **cloud platforms** like **Heroku**, **AWS EC2**, or **Google Cloud**:

- For **Heroku**, you can deploy a Flask or Django app with a **Procfile** and a `requirements.txt`.
- For **AWS EC2**, you can host your Dockerized app and set up an **Nginx** reverse proxy for production.

Step 4: Model Update Strategy

If the model needs to be updated, you can:

- **Retrain the model** periodically and deploy new versions.
- Use **A/B testing** to compare the old and new model's performance in production.

Conclusion

In this chapter, you learned: **How to integrate Flask and Django with TensorFlow and PyTorch** to build AI-powered applications. **How to build image classification, sentiment analysis, and recommendation system apps**. **How to deploy machine learning models with Flask and Django APIs** in a production environment using Docker and cloud platforms.

By combining machine learning and AI with web frameworks like **Flask** and **Django**, you can create powerful, real-time, intelligent applications that offer dynamic user experiences.

CHAPTER 25

FUTURE TRENDS AND CAREER OPPORTUNITIES IN WEB DEVELOPMENT

Web development is a fast-evolving field, and staying updated with the latest trends and career opportunities is crucial for anyone aspiring to build a long-term career in the industry. Python web frameworks like **Django** and **Flask** have become cornerstones in web development, and they are continually adapting to meet the demands of modern applications.

In this chapter, we'll explore:
The future of Python web frameworks
How to become a professional Django/Flask developer
Learning paths and job opportunities

25.1 The Future of Python Web Frameworks

25.1.1 Increased Demand for Real-Time and Asynchronous Applications

As real-time applications become more prevalent, the demand for web frameworks that support **asynchronous programming** and **real-time communication** is growing. Python web frameworks, including **Django Channels** for Django and **Flask-SocketIO** for Flask, have integrated support for **WebSockets**, which enables developers to build **chat applications**, **live notifications**, and **collaborative platforms**. As demand for these applications increases, we can expect Python frameworks to continue improving their real-time and asynchronous capabilities.

25.1.2 Serverless and Microservices Architecture

With the rise of **serverless computing** and **microservices architecture**, web frameworks are evolving to integrate easily with these modern application deployment patterns. Both Flask and Django are becoming more **lightweight** and **modular**, allowing them to work seamlessly in **serverless environments** (like AWS Lambda) and be part of **microservices architectures**. Expect further growth in tools and best practices around serverless deployments in the Python web framework ecosystem.

25.1.3 Improved Integration with Frontend Technologies

Modern web applications demand seamless integration between frontend frameworks (like **React**, **Vue.js**, and **Angular**) and backend services. Frameworks like Django and Flask are improving their support for these **single-page applications (SPAs)**. **Django Rest Framework (DRF)** and **GraphQL** integration are already making it easier to build powerful, data-driven apps. As JavaScript frameworks continue to dominate the frontend, expect better support and improved workflows for building full-stack web apps in Python.

25.1.4 Enhanced Security Features

Security is always a top priority, and the future of Python web frameworks will focus on improving built-in security features. Frameworks like Django already offer robust protection against common threats like **CSRF**, **XSS**, and **SQL injection**. Going forward, these frameworks will continue to integrate advanced security mechanisms, ensuring better protection out of the box and addressing emerging vulnerabilities in web applications.

25.1.5 Artificial Intelligence and Machine Learning Integration

With the rise of **AI and ML** in various industries, Python's web frameworks are poised to become more AI-driven. We've seen frameworks like Django and Flask integrate well with machine learning libraries like **TensorFlow** and **PyTorch**. The future will see even deeper integration of AI technologies in Python web frameworks, enabling developers to build smarter, more personalized applications that can analyze data, make decisions, and interact with users in new ways.

25.2 How to Become a Professional Django/Flask Developer

25.2.1 Mastering the Fundamentals

Before diving into advanced concepts, it's important to master the **core principles** of web development and Python programming. These include:

- **HTTP Protocol**: Understand how web browsers and servers communicate.
- **Databases**: Learn SQL and understand how to work with relational databases like **PostgreSQL** and **MySQL**.
- **Web Servers**: Understand how web servers like **Nginx** and **Apache** work with web frameworks.

25.2.2 Learning Django and Flask

Django

To become proficient in Django, you should:

- Start with the official **Django documentation** and build basic projects like a **blog** or **to-do app**.
- Learn how to build RESTful APIs using **Django REST Framework (DRF)**.
- Understand **Django's ORM** for managing databases and relationships.
- Explore Django's advanced features, like **custom middleware**, **signals**, and **authentication**.

Flask

To master Flask, you should:

- Start by building basic **Flask applications**, such as a **simple blog** or a **REST API**.

281

- Understand **Flask extensions**, like **Flask-SQLAlchemy**, **Flask-WTF**, and **Flask-Login**.
- Learn how to work with **Flask's routing system**, templates, and session management.
- Understand how to scale Flask applications using **blueprints**, **factories**, and integrating with **Redis** or **Celery** for background tasks.

25.2.3 Building Real-World Projects

Hands-on experience is essential in becoming a professional Django or Flask developer. Start by working on real-world projects that involve:

- **User authentication** (login, registration, password reset)
- **File handling** (upload and manage images, videos, etc.)
- **Building REST APIs** for communication between the frontend and backend
- **Integration with third-party services** (like payment gateways, APIs, etc.)

Additionally, contributing to **open-source projects** related to Django or Flask can be a great way to gain exposure to best practices and collaborate with other developers.

25.2.4 Learning Deployment and DevOps Skills

Professional developers need to know how to deploy applications to production. Learn how to:

- Deploy Django/Flask applications on **Heroku**, **AWS EC2**, **DigitalOcean**, or **Docker** containers.
- Configure **CI/CD pipelines** (using tools like **GitHub Actions**, **Jenkins**, or **GitLab CI**) for automated testing and deployment.
- Understand how to monitor and maintain your application once it's live (e.g., using **New Relic**, **Sentry**, or **Prometheus**).

25.2.5 Stay Updated

Web development is a constantly evolving field. Follow industry blogs, listen to podcasts, and attend conferences or webinars to stay up to date with the latest trends and tools. Here are some useful resources:

- **Django and Flask documentation**: Always the first place to check for updates.
- **Real Python**: A great platform for tutorials and articles on Python web development.
- **PyCon**: An annual Python conference that often covers Django and Flask topics.

25.3 Learning Paths and Job Opportunities

25.3.1 Learning Paths

Here is a suggested **learning path** for becoming a skilled Django/Flask developer:

1. **Step   1:   Learn   Python**
   Master the basics of Python, including data structures, object-oriented programming, and libraries like **requests**, **BeautifulSoup**, and **SQLAlchemy**.

2. **Step 2: Master Web Development Basics**
   Understand **HTML, CSS**, and **JavaScript**. Learn about **HTTP, RESTful APIs**, and **WebSockets**.

3. **Step   3:   Learn   Django   or   Flask**
   Start with building simple apps. Gradually build more complex applications that require **authentication**, **data storage**, and **third-party integration**.

4. **Step   4:   Explore   Advanced   Features**
   Learn about **database optimization, caching, background tasks**, and **security best practices**.

5. **Step   5:   Build   Real-World   Projects**
   Focus on practical projects like **e-commerce sites**,

blog platforms, or **task management apps**. Make sure to incorporate **unit testing, debugging**, and **deployment**.

6. **Step 6: Contribute to Open-Source Projects**
Contributing to open-source projects can help you learn best practices and gain visibility within the developer community.

25.3.2 Job Opportunities

As a Django/Flask developer, you have a wide array of job opportunities in the web development and software engineering space.

Job Roles:

- **Backend Developer**: Develop the server-side logic, APIs, and databases for web applications.
- **Full-Stack Developer**: Work on both the frontend (React/Vue) and backend (Django/Flask).
- **API Developer**: Focus on building and maintaining RESTful APIs or GraphQL services.
- **DevOps Engineer**: Work on deployment pipelines, automation, and managing the infrastructure for Django/Flask apps.

Companies Hiring:

- **Tech Startups**: Many startups are adopting Django and Flask for quick prototyping and building scalable web applications.
- **E-commerce Platforms**: Companies like **Shopify**, **Etsy**, and **Amazon** use Django to handle large-scale transactions and user management.
- **Consulting Firms**: Many consultancies hire Django/Flask developers for client-based web application projects.

Conclusion

In this chapter, you learned:
The future trends of Python web frameworks, such as Django and Flask, including real-time applications, microservices, and AI integration.
How to become a professional Django/Flask developer, focusing on mastering the basics, building real-world projects, and learning deployment and DevOps.
Career opportunities and learning paths to help you become a well-rounded developer and take advantage of job openings in the web development field.

The world of web development is vast and constantly evolving, and Django and Flask will continue to be key players in building modern, scalable web applications. By mastering these frameworks, you'll be well-positioned to take on exciting projects and career opportunities in the future.